ProMgmt.®

Professional Cooking

FIFTH EDITION

Student Workbook

National Restaurant Association
EDUCATIONAL FOUNDATION

JOHN WILEY & SONS, INC.

ProMgmt. is a registered trademark of the National Restaurant Association Educational Foundation.

This student workbook is designed to be used with the textbook *Professional Cooking, Fifth Edition* by Wayne Gisslen.

This book is printed on acid-free paper. ∞

Published by John Wiley & Sons, Inc., New York

Published simultaneously in Canada.

This publication is designed to provide accurate and authoritative information in regard to the subject matter covered. It is sold with the understanding that the publisher is not engaged in rendering professional services. If professional advice or other expert assistance is required, the services of a competent professional should be sought.

Wiley also publishes its books in a variety of electronic formats. Some content that appears in print may not be available in electronic books. For more information about Wiley products, visit our web site at www.wiley.com.

Library of Congress Cataloging-in-Publication Data:

ISBN: 0-471-20881-7

Printed in the United States of America

10 9 8 7 6 5 4

Contents

INTRODUCTION

The respect and high regard shown to great chefs is certainly well deserved. It takes years of careful study, training, and experience to achieve success as a professional cook.

Professional Cooking, Fifth Edition, is intended as a comprehensive overview of the chef's art for the foodservice manager. This course will provide a foundation of fundamental knowledge upon which to build your menu and to supervise your kitchen.

The ProMgmt.® Program

How to Earn a ProMgmt. Certificate of Course Completion

To earn a ProMgmt. Certificate of Course Completion, a student must complete all student workbook exercises and receive a passing score on the final examination.

To apply for the ProMgmt. Certificate of Course Completion, complete the student registration form located on the inside back cover of this workbook and give it to your instructor, who will then forward it to the National Restaurant Association Educational Foundation.

Each student registered with the NRAEF will receive a student number. Please make a record of it; this number will identify you during your present and future coursework with the NRAEF.

ProMgmt. certificate requirements are administered exclusively through colleges and other educational institutions that offer ProMgmt. courses and examinations.

If you are not currently enrolled in a ProMgmt. course and would like to earn a ProMgmt. certificate, please contact your local educational institution to see if they are willing to administer the ProMgmt. certificate requirements for non-enrolled students. You can also visit www.nraef.org for a list of ProMgmt. Partner schools. ProMgmt. Partner schools offer seven or more courses that include administration of the ProMgmt. certificate requirements.

The NRAEF leaves it to the discretion of each educational institution offering ProMgmt. courses to decide whether or not that institution will administer the ProMgmt. certificate requirements to non-enrolled students. If an institution does administer ProMgmt. certificate requirements to non-enrolled students, that institution may charge an additional fee, of an amount determined by that institution, for the administration of the ProMgmt. certificate requirements.

Course Materials

This course consists of the text, *Professional Cooking, Fifth Edition,* by Wayne Gisslen, the student workbook, and a final examination. The examination is the final section of your course and is sent to an instructor for administration, then returned to the NRAEF for grading.

Each chapter consists of:

- Learning Objectives
- Chapter Study Outline
- Chapter Check-in
- Answers to Chapter Check-in (at the end of the workbook)

At the end of the workbook you will find:

- An 80-question practice test
- Answers to the practice test

The objectives indicate what you can expect to learn from the course, and are designed to help you organize your studying and concentrate on important topics and explanations. Refer to the objectives frequently to make sure you are meeting them.

The exercises help you check how well you've learned the concepts in each chapter. These will be graded by your instructor.

An 80-question Practice Test appears at the end of the workbook. All the questions are multiple-choice and have four possible answers. Circle the best answer to each question, as in this example:

Who was the first president of the United States?
A. Thomas Jefferson
B. *George Washington*
C. Benjamin Franklin
D. John Adams

Answers to the Practice Test follow in the workbook so that you can grade your own work.

The Final Exam

All examinations can first be graded by your instructor and then officially graded again by the NRAEF. If you do not receive a passing grade on the examination, you may request a retest. A retest fee will be charged for the second examination.

Study Tips

Since you have already demonstrated an interest in furthering your foodservice education by registering for this NRAEF course, you know that your next step is study preparation. We have included some specific study aids that you might find useful.

-   Build studying time into your routine. If you hold a full-time job, you need to take a realistic approach to studying. Set aside a specific time and place to study, and stick to your routine as closely as possible. Your study area should have room for your course materials and any other necessary study aids. If possible, your area should be away from family traffic.
-   Discuss with family members your study goals and your need for a quiet place and private time to work. They might want to help you draw up a study schedule that will be satisfactory to everyone.
-   Keep a study log. You can record what chapter was worked on, a list of topics studied, the time you put in, and how well you scored on the Chapter Check-ins and Practice Text.
-   Work at your own pace, but move ahead steadily. The following tips should help you get the most value from your lessons.
    1. Look over the objectives carefully. They list what you are expected to know for the examination.

2. Read the chapters carefully, and don't hesitate to mark your text—it will help you later. Mark passages that seem especially important and those that seem difficult, as you might want to reread them later.
3. Try to read an entire chapter at a time. Even though more than one chapter might be assigned at time, you might find you can carefully read only one chapter in a sitting.
4. When you have finished reading the chapter, go back and check the highlights and any notes you have made. These will help you review for the examination.

Reviewing for the Final Exam

Once you have completed the final exercise and Practice Test, you will have several items to use for your examination review. If you have highlighted important points in the textbook, you can review them. If you have made notes in the margins, check them to be sure you have answered any questions that arose when you read the material. Reread certain sections if necessary. Finally, you should go over your exercises.

The ProMgmt.® Program

The National Restaurant Association Educational Foundation's ProMgmt. program is designed to provide foodservice students and professionals with a solid foundation of practical knowledge and information. Each course focuses on a specific management area. Students who earn ProMgmt. certificates improve their chances of:
- Earning NRAEF Undergraduate Scholarships.
- Gaining management jobs within the foodservice and restaurant industry.

For more information on both the ProMgmt. program and scholarships, please contact the NRAEF at 800.765.2122 (312.715.1010 in Chicagoland), or visit our Web site at **www.nraef.org**.

CHAPTER 1

Learning Objectives

After reading this chapter, you should be able to:

1.1   Name and describe four major developments that have significantly changed the food service industry in the 20th century.

1.2   Identify seven major stations in a classical kitchen.

1.3   Explain how the size and type of an operation influence the organization of the modern kitchen.

1.4   Identify and describe three skill levels of food production personnel

1.5   Identify eight behavioral characteristics that food service workers should develop and maintain to achieve the highest standards of professionalism.

Chapter 1 Study Outline

1. Modern food service grew out of, and is primarily based on, the European tradition.
    - Modern food service began when the 1793 French Revolution ended the monarchy, spurring great chefs formerly employed in the houses of the nobility to open restaurants.

2. Considered the founder of the classical European-based cuisine, **Marie-Antoine Carême** organized and refined cooking techniques.
    - His books contain the first systematic records of culinary principles and techniques, recipes, and menu development.
    - Carême also developed elaborate, elegant display pieces on which modern wedding cakes and other culinary works are based.

3. **Auguste Escoffier** is considered the father of twentieth-century cookery.
    - He simplified menus and streamlined the organization of kitchen work into stations or departments, forming the basis for today's systems.

4. Twentieth-century technological and social developments have changed food production methods and food preferences.

   - Electric- and gas-powered refrigeration, preparation, and cooking equipment have simplified production, provided better control over processes, and allowed for variability in timing of production stages, including advance preparation.

   - Food handling and eating habits have changed because refrigeration and rapid transportation make fresh foods produced anywhere available everywhere all year. Additionally, preservation techniques have increased availability and have made formerly rare and expensive foods more affordable.

   - Convenience foods have been developed.

   - New, widespread knowledge of nutrition and foodborne illnesses has changed food handling and customer demands.

5. A kitchen is organized based on the menu, the type of establishment, the size of the operation, and the physical facilities.

6. The major positions in the modern foodservice system are the chef, the sous chef, the station chefs, and the cooks and assistants.

   - The chef is in charge of the kitchen.

   - The sous chef is directly in charge of production.

   - Station chefs include the sauce chef, the fish cook, the vegetable cook, the roast cook, the pantry chef, the pastry chef, and the relief cook.

7. Foodservice workers need a variety of skills.

   - Entry level employees usually need no skills; most gain promotable skills on the job.

   - A person in a supervisory position needs good knowledge and experience in food production; organizing skills; human resources management skills; and planning, budgeting, and cost control abilities.

6. The professional foodservice worker should have a positive attitude toward the job, staying power, an ability to work with people, an eagerness to learn, a full range of skills, experience, dedication to quality, and a good understanding of the basics of cooking.

Chapter 1 Exercises

1. Match each kitchen position on the left with its description on the right.

_____(1) Executive chef

_____(2) Sous chef

_____(3) Station chef

_____(4) Working chef

_____(5) Sauce chef

_____(6) Short-order cook

_____(7) Pantry chef

_____(8) Cook

a. Responsible for cold foods, including salads and dressings, pâtés, cold hors d'oeuvres, and buffet items

b. Prepares sauces, stews, and hot hors d'oeuvres; sautés foods to order

c. Kitchen manager responsible for all aspects of food preparation

d. In charge of particular areas of production

e. Directly in charge of production and minute-by-minute supervision of staff

f. Helps with specific duties as assigned

g. In charge of a smaller kitchen and usually heads one production station

h. Responsible for the preparation of food that can be quickly prepared to order

L.O. 1.2

2. Give 3 examples of institutional food service.

- _____

- _____

- _____

L.O. 1.3

3. What are some of the qualities that a professional foodservice worker must have?

_____

_____

_____

L.O. 1.5

4. If you consider the French meaning of the word "chef," what is the difference between a cook and a chef?

_____

_____

_____

L.O. 1.2

5. List 5 duties or responsibilities of an executive chef besides cooking.

- _____

- _____

- _____

- _____

- _____

L.O. 1.2

Chapter 1 Check-in

1. Which of the following does the sauce chef prepare as part of his or her duties?

    A. Roasted meats
    B. Sautéed meats
    C. Vegetable side dishes
    D. Broiled meats

    L.O. 1.2

2. A professional food service worker should have a(n)

    A. positive attitude toward the job.
    B. eagerness to learn.
    C. ability to work with people.
    D. All of the above are correct.

    L.O. 1.5

3. Which of the following cooks is least likely to handle meat products as part of his or her duties?

    A. Sauce cook
    B. Pantry cook
    C. Vegetable cook
    D. Grill cook

    L.O. 1.2

4. Which of the following developments has not had a major effect on the food service industry in the twentieth and twenty-first centuries?

    A. Increased understanding of sanitation
    B. Development of refrigeration equipment
    C. Development of modern transportation systems
    D. All of the above are correct.

    L.O. 1.1

5. The term "chef" refers to a

    A. person in charge of a kitchen or part of a kitchen.
    B. professional cook.
    C. cook who prepares gourmet foods.
    D. person who has completed a course of study in an accredited professional cooking school.

    L.O. 1.4

CHAPTER 2

SANITATION AND SAFETY

Learning Objectives

After reading this chapter, you should be able to:

2.1   Describe steps to prevent food poisoning and foodborne diseases in the following areas: personal hygiene; food handling and storage techniques; cleaning and sanitizing procedures; and pest control.

2.2   Identify safe workplace habits that prevent injuries from the following: cuts, burns, operation of machinery and equipment, and lifting.

2.3   Identify safe workplace habits that minimize the likelihood of fires and falls.

Chapter 2 Study Outline

1. Bacteria can be harmless, beneficial, undesirable, or can cause disease.
   - Beneficial bacteria can aid digestion while others allow for the manufacture of yogurt, cheese, and other products.
   - Undesirable bacteria can cause food spoilage and might or might not cause disease. Their presence can be detected in food by color change, odor, or slimy surfaces.
   - Pathogens (disease-causing bacteria) might not be detectable. The only protection from these pathogens is proper handling and storage of foods.

2. Bacteria require six elements in which to grow and thrive:
   - Food
   - Moisture
   - Warm temperatures of 40°F to 140°F (4.4°C to 60°C)
   - Neutral acid/alkaline environment
   - Air (aerobic bacteria) or no air (anaerobic bacteria)
   - Time

3. Bacteria are spread by human hands, coughs, sneezes, air, water, insects, rodents, and by equipment, utensils, and other foods.

4. There are three principles of food protection against bacteria.
   - Keep bacteria from spreading.
   - Stop bacteria from growing.
   - Kill bacteria.
5. Diseases caused by bacteria can be **intoxications** or **infections**.
   - The most common foodborne diseases are botulism, staph, e. coli, salmonella, clostridium perfringens, streptococcal, infectious hepatitis, and trichinosis.
6. Chemical poisoning can be caused by defective or improper equipment, exposure of foods to various chemicals, and contamination of food with objects that might not be toxic but might cause injury or discomfort.
7. Bacteria spread by food workers cause most foodborne disease.
8. The first step in foodborne disease prevention is good personal hygiene.
9. The overall goals of food storage rules and methods are to prevent growth of bacteria already in foods and to prevent contamination.
   - Design dry food storage to keep out insects, rodents, dirt, moisture, and sometimes air.
   - Frozen foods should be kept at 0°F (–17.8°C) or lower, tightly wrapped, and labeled.
   - Refrigerator temperature should be no higher than 40°F (4.4°C).
   - Hot food holding equipment should keep food above 140°F (60°C). Food should be preheated before placed in holding equipment.
10. Sanitation problems in food handling and preparation include the danger of cross-contamination and the problem of having items at "food danger zone" temperatures while working with them.
11. Cleaning and sanitizing equipment are vital in food service.
    - **Cleaning** means removing visible soil; **sanitizing** means killing disease-causing bacteria.
    - Bacteria can be killed by heat or by chemicals.
    - Both manual and mechanical dishwashing require the following procedure: scrape and prerinse, wash, rinse, sanitize, drain, and air dry.
12. Methods of controlling rodents and insects include eliminating their places of entry to the building; eliminating spaces and conditions in the building that provide hiding and breeding places; eliminating their sources of food; and extermination.
13. The **HACCP** system uses critical control points to fight contamination.
    - The flow of food through the organization goes from receiving to the consumer.
    - At each **critical control point**—a step where there is a risk of potentially hazardous food—it is possible to take some action to eliminate or reduce the hazard.
14. Foodservice safety focuses on preventing cuts, burns, fires, equipment injuries, falls, and lifting injuries.

Chapter 2 Exercises

1. List and briefly discuss the three basic principles of food protection against bacteria.

   • _____

   _____

   • _____

   _____

   • _____

   _____

L.O. 2.1

2. Most disease-causing bacteria require moisture to grow. Indicate which of the following foods are most likely to be potentially hazardous.

   _____Whole-wheat bread   _____Rye crackers

   _____Macaroni salad   _____Raw eggs

   _____Melon   _____Powdered pancake mix

   _____Popcorn   _____Fresh pasta

   _____Uncooked rice   _____Milk

L.O. 2.1

3. Most disease-causing bacteria require a neutral environment—neither too acidic nor too alkaline—in order to grow. Indicate which of the following foods are most likely to be potentially hazardous.

   _____Guacamole   _____Hard-cooked eggs

   _____Grapefruit   _____Mayonnaise

   _____Chicken   _____Mustard

   _____Lemon juice   _____Ice cream

   _____Tomatoes   _____Milk

L.O. 2.1

4. Match each foodborne disease on the left with the food on the right with which it is most often associated. Letters may be used more than once.

_____(1) Botulism
_____(2) Staphylococcus
_____(3) E. coli
_____(4) Salmonella
_____(5) Clostridium perfringens
_____(6) Trichinosis

a. Undercooked pork
b. Canned foods
c. High-protein foods

L.O. 2.1

5. In the HACCP system, what is a critical control point?

_____

_____

_____

L.O. 2.1

6. Explain why each of the following is an unsafe practice.
   (1) Wearing short sleeves while cooking

   _____

   _____

   (2) Using a damp towel to grab a hot pan's handle

   _____

   _____

   (3) Putting icy or wet foods in a deep-fat fryer

   _____

   _____

   (4) Lifting a pot lid toward you

   _____

   _____

   (5) Turning on a gas burner and then lighting a match

   _____

   _____

L.O. 2.2

7. Which are safer, sharp or dull knives? Why?

_____

_____

_____

L.O. 2.3

8. Match each material on the left with the class of fires on the right to which it belongs. Letters may be used more than once.

_____(1) Cloth apron   a.   Class A

_____(2) Television set   b.   Class B

_____(3) Paper napkins   c.   Class C

_____(4) Hot fat

_____(5) Kerosene

_____(6) Photocopy machine

_____(7) Wood cutting board

_____(8) Cooking grease

L.O. 2.3

9. What two common kitchen ingredients can be used to put out stove-top fires?

• _____

• _____

L.O. 2.3

10. With which part of the body should you lift heavy objects?

_____

L.O. 2.2

Chapter 2 Check-in

1. Which of the following statements about bacteria is true?

    A. Bacteria multiply by splitting in half.
    B. Bacteria can double in number every 15 to 30 seconds.
    C. A single bacterium can multiply to a million in 30 minutes.
    D. All of the above are correct.

    L.O. 2.1

2. There are three basic principles of protecting food from bacteria. Which of the following is not one of them?

    A. Kill bacteria.
    B. Stop bacteria from growing.
    C. Promote the locomotion of bacteria.
    D. Keep bacteria from spreading.

    L.O. 2.1

3. Which of the following is most responsible for spreading bacteria that cause foodborne disease?

    A. Food workers
    B. Insects
    C. Rodents
    D. Dirty equipment

    L.O. 2.1

4. Which of the following is an example of physical contamination?

    A. Cyanide from silver polish
    B. Piece of glass from a broken container
    C. Insect parts
    D. Trichinosis organisms in meat

    L.O. 2.1

5. Which of the following is a correct safety rule for avoiding cuts?

    A. Avoid using knives that are too sharp.
    B. Do not soak knives by putting them in the sink and covering them with soapy water.
    C. If you drop a knife from the workbench, try to catch it before it falls on your foot.
    D. When you carry a knife, hold it in front of you with the blade pointed away from yourself.

    L.O. 2.2

CHAPTER 3

TOOLS AND EQUIPMENT

Learning Objectives
After reading this chapter, you should be able to:

3.1   Identify the do's and don'ts associated with the safe and efficient use of standard cooking equipment; processing equipment; holding and storage equipment; measuring devices; and knives, hand tools, and small equipment.

Chapter 3 Study Outline

1. Foodservice establishments use a variety of cooking equipment.
    - Cook tops can be open elements, flat top (lightweight), heavy-duty flat top, or induction.
    - Among the ovens available are conventional ovens, convection ovens, revolving ovens, slow-cook-and-hold ovens, combination steamer ovens, barbecue or smoke ovens, infrared or reconstituting ovens, and microwave ovens.
    - Overhead broilers generate heat from above; salamanders are small broilers used primarily for browning or glazing the tops of some items.
    - On grills, the heat source is below the grid that holds the food.
    - Griddles are flat, smooth, heated surfaces on which food is cooked directly.
    - Rotisseries cook foods by turning them slowly in front of heating elements.
    - Deep fryers cook foods in hot fat.
    - Versatile and efficient, the tilting skillet is a shallow, flat-bottomed pot.
    - Steam-jacketed kettles heat quickly and have uniform and controllable heat.
    - Steam cookers cook foods rapidly and with minimum loss of nutrients and flavor.

2. Processing equipment includes mixers, food cutters, slicers, and VCMs.
   - Vertical mixers are useful for a variety of food mixing and processing jobs.
   - The food cutter is used for general food chopping.
   - Among the attachments for mixers and food choppers are the food grinder, the slicer/shredder, and the dicer.
   - Slicers slice foods more evenly and uniformly than can be done by hand.
   - The vertical cutter/mixer (VCM) is used to chop and mix large quantities of foods rapidly.
3. Holding and storage equipment is available for both hot and cold food.
   - Hot food should be held above 140°F (60°C) to prevent the growth of bacteria.
     - Steam tables are standard equipment for serving lines.
     - A bain marie is a hot-water bath.
     - Overhead infrared lamps keep plated food warm.
   - Cold food should be kept in refrigerators below 40°F (4.4°C) or in freezers in order to prevent bacterial growth.
     - Items should be placed so that air can circulate.
     - The unit's door should be kept closed as much as possible.
     - Foods should be well wrapped.
     - Refrigerators should be kept clean.
4. The factors that affect a pan's ability to cook evenly are the thickness of the metal and the kind of metal used.
   - Aluminum is used for most cooking utensils.
   - Copper is the best heat conductor.
   - Stainless steel is ideal for storage containers.
   - Cast iron distributes heat evenly and maintains high temperatures for long periods.
   - Porcelain enamel-lined pans scratch and chip easily.
   - No-stick plastic-type coatings provide a slippery finish.
   - Glass and earthenware are very breakable.
5. Pots and pans come in a variety of shapes and sizes, each made for several specific uses or jobs.
6. Devices used for measuuring include scales, volume measures, measuring cups, measuring spoons, ladles, scoops, and thermometers.

7. Food workers have a number of knives and hand tools at their disposal.
   - Knives are made of carbon steel, stainless steel, or high-carbon stainless steel.
     - The French knife is the one most frequently used in the kitchen.
     - Other knives include the utility, paring, boning, butcher, steak, oyster, and clam knives; the slicer; the cleaver; and the vegetable peeler.
   - Hand tools include the melon ball scoop, cook's fork, spatula, spreader, pie server, and pastry wheel.

Chapter 3 Exercises

1. Match each oven type on the left with its description on the right.

   _____(1) Conventional oven

   _____(2) Convection oven

   _____(3) Revolving oven

   _____(4) Slow-cook-and-hold oven

   _____(5) Combination steamer oven

   _____(6) Barbecue or smoke oven

   _____(7) Infrared or reconstituting oven

   _____(8) Microwave oven

   a. Cooks food by radiation generated by special tubes

   b. Produces wood smoke that surrounds and flavors food as it bakes or roasts

   c. Uses electronic controls and probes that cook food at steady temperatures and allow for holding of food

   d. Uses quartz tubes that bring large quantities of food to serving temperature in a short time

   e. Operates by heating air in an enclosed space

   f. Can be operated in three different modes: as a convection oven, a convection steamer, or a high-humidity oven

   g. Contains fans that circulate air and distribute heat rapidly

   h. Contains many shelves and trays on a Ferris-wheel-type attachment

L.O. 3.1

2. Which type of cooking equipment:
   a. gives food a charcoal or smoky flavor?

   _____

   b. cooks food slowly by turning it in front of a heat source?

   _____

L.O. 3.1

14

3. Match each piece of equipment on the left with its primary use on the right.

_____(1) Bain marie
_____(2) VCM
_____(3) China cap
_____(4) Hot top
_____(5) Salamander

a. Broiling or browning
b. Chopping, mixing, puréeing
c. Holding hot foods
d. Range-top cooking
e. Straining foods

L.O. 3.1

4. Indicate both an advantage and disadvantage associated with each metal below.

A   D
____ ____(1) Aluminum
____ ____(2) Copper
____ ____(3) Stainless steel
____ ____(4) Cast iron
____ ____(5) Teflon

Advantages:
a. Conducts heat very well
b. Nonstick
c. Good for storing foods
d. Lightweight
e. Maintains high temperatures for long periods

Disadvantages:
f. Very heavy
g. Reacts with high-acid foods in storage
h. Conducts heat poorly
i. Scratches or cracks easily
j. Very expensive

L.O. 3.1

5. Match each pot or pan on the left with its description on the right.

_____(1) Stock pot
_____(2) Brazier
_____(3) Saucepan
_____(4) Sauté pan
_____(5) Cast iron skillet
_____(6) Double boiler
_____(7) Sheet pan

a. Round, shallow pan used to brown, braise, and stew meats
b. Lower section of this two-sectioned pan holds boiling water
c. Very heavy pan used for pan-frying
d. Large pot used to simmer liquids
e. Used to cook foods quickly over high heat
f. All-purpose pan with one long handle
g. Shallow, rectangular pan for baking cakes

L.O. 3.1

6. Match each knife on the left with its primary use on the right.

_____(1) French knife
_____(2) Utility knife
_____(3) Paring knife
_____(4) Serrated knife
_____(5) Butcher knife
_____(6) Cleaver

a. Cutting through bones
b. Trimming fruits and vegetables
c. All-purpose slicing, chopping, etc.
d. Cutting breads and cakes
e. Trimming and cutting raw meats
f. Cutting and preparing pantry items

L.O. 3.1

7. Describe the difference between the following items.

(1) Solid, slotted, and perforated spoons

_____

_____

_____

(2) Strainer and colander

_____

_____

(3) Heavy whip and balloon whip

_____

_____

L.O. 3.1

Chapter 3 Check-in

1. Which of the following is not one of the basic types of range tops?

   A. Microwave
   B. Induction
   C. Open burner
   D. Heavy-duty flat top

   L.O. 3.1

2. Which of the following types of deep fryers cooks food the fastest?

   A. Pressure fryer
   B. Automatic fryer
   C. Radiant fryer
   D. Standard deep fryer

   L.O. 3.1

3. Which type of equipment heats from the sides as well as from the bottom?

   A. Steam cooker
   B. Pressure cooker
   C. Convection cooker
   D. Steam kettle

L.O. 3.1

4. Which of the following is best suited for cooking in a pressure steamer?

   A. Soup
   B. Vegetables
   C. Meats
   D. Breads

L.O. 3.1

5. What kind of thermometer can register the highest temperature?

   A. Meat thermometer
   B. Fat thermometer
   C. Instant-read thermometer
   D. Hotel thermometer

L.O. 3.1

CHAPTER 4

BASIC COOKING PRINCIPLES

Learning Objectives

After reading this chapter, you should be able to:

4.1   Name the most important components of foods and describe what happens to them when they are cooked.

4.2   Name and describe the three ways in which heat is transferred to food in order to cook it.

4.3   List three factors that affect cooking times.

4.4   Explain the differences between moist-heat cooking methods, dry-heat cooking methods, and dry-heat cooking methods using fat.

4.5   Describe each basic cooking method used in the commercial kitchen.

4.6   Identify five properties that determine the quality of a deep-fried product.

4.7   Explain the difference between a seasoning and a flavoring ingredient and give examples of each.

4.8   Identify appropriate times for adding seasoning ingredients to the cooking process in order to achieve optimal results.

4.9   Identify appropriate times for adding flavoring ingredients to the cooking process in order to achieve optimal results.

4.10   List eleven guidelines for using herbs and spices in cooking.

Chapter 4 Study Outline

1. The components of food react differently when exposed to heat during cooking.
   - Proteins become firm, or coagulate, and lose moisture.
   - Carbohydrates **caramelize** (sugars brown) or **gelatinize** (starches absorb water and swell).
   - Fruit and vegetable fiber breaks down as fruits and vegetables soften.
   - Fats break down and, when hot enough, deteriorate rapidly and begin to smoke.

2. The three methods of heat transfer are:
   - Conduction
   - Convection
   - Radiation

3. The best choice of cooking method(s) for a specific food item depends on its softness or firmness, amount of fiber or connective tissue, delicacy of flavor, and many other considerations.

4. Methods in which heat is conducted to food by water or by steam are **moist-heat methods**. These include:
   - Boiling
   - Simmering
   - Poaching
   - Blanching
   - Steaming
   - Braising

5. Methods in which heat is transferred without moisture—by hot air, hot metal, radiation, or hot fat—are **dry-heat methods**. These include:
   - Roasting
   - Baking
   - Barbecuing
   - Smoke-roasting
   - Broiling
   - Grilling
   - Griddling
   - Pan-broiling
   - Sautéing
   - Pan-frying
   - Deep-frying

6. Microwave ovens are used for primary cooking, heating prepared foods, and thawing raw or cooked items.

7. **Seasoning** enhances the natural flavor of food; **flavoring** is defined as adding a new flavor to food.

8. **Herbs** are the leaves of certain plants; **spices** are the buds, fruits, flowers, bark, seeds, and roots of plants and trees.

Chapter 4 Exercises

1. A cook has deep-fried some potatoes, but they are excessively greasy. Explain why this might have happened.

   _____

   _____

   _____

L.O. 4.6

2. You are preparing a plate of baked chicken breast and steamed broccoli for reheating in the microwave oven. Describe how you should arrange the food on the plate so that all items are cooked thoroughly.

   _____

   _____

   _____

L.O. 4.5

3. Explain the difference between each of the following terms.
   (1) Conduction and convection

   _____

   _____

   _____

   (2) Caramelization and gelatinization

   _____

   _____

   _____

   (3) Seasoning and flavoring

   _____

   _____

   _____

L.O. 4.1, 4.2, 4.7

4. Indicate whether each cooking method below is a moist-heat (M) or a dry-heat (D) method.

_____(1)   Boil

_____(2)   Broil

_____(3)   Sauté

_____(4)   Pan-broil

_____(5)   Deep-fry

_____(6)   Braise

_____(7)   Roast

_____(8)   Bake

_____(9)   Grill

_____(10)   Poach

_____(11)   Pan-fry

_____(12)   Steam

_____(13)   Simmer

_____(14)   Blanch

_____(15)   Barbecue

_____(16)   Griddle

L.O. 4.4

5. Indicate whether each of the following is an herb (H) or a spice (S).

_____(1)   Allspice

_____(2)   Anise seed

_____(3)   Basil

_____(4)   Bay leaf

_____(5)   Caraway seed

_____(6)   Cardamom

_____(7)   Cayenne

_____(8)   Celery seed

_____(9)   Chervil

_____(10)   Chili powder

_____(11)   Chive

_____(12)   Cinnamon

_____(13)   Clove

_____(14)   Coriander

_____(15)   Cumin

_____(16)   Curry powder

_____(17)   Dill

_____(18)   Fennel

_____(19)   Marjoram

_____(20)   Mint

_____(21)   Mustard seed

_____(22)   Nutmeg

_____(23)   Oregano

_____(24)   Paprika

_____(25)   Parsley

_____(26)   Pepper (black, white, or red)

_____(27)   Poppy seed

_____(28)   Rosemary

_____(29)   Saffron

_____(30)   Sage

_____(31)   Savory

_____(32)   Sesame seed

_____(33)   Tarragon

_____(34)   Thyme

_____(35)   Turmeric

L.O. 4.10

6. What are the three main factors that affect cooking times?

- _____
- _____
- _____

L.O. 4.3

Chapter 4 Check-in

1. What effect does acid have when it is added to meat during cooking?

   A. It speeds up the process of gelatinization.
   B. It helps to dissolve some of the connective tissue.
   C. It slows the process of coagulation.
   D. It raises the smoke point.

   L.O. 4.1

2. The heat transfer method by which heat is transferred directly from one item to an item touching it is called

   A. convection.
   B. radiation.
   C. transferal.
   D. conduction.

   L.O. 4.2

3. The heat transfer method by which heat is transferred from part of an object to another part of the same object is called

   A. convection.
   B. radiation.
   C. transferal.
   D. conduction.

   L.O. 4.2

4. The time it takes a food to be cooked to doneness is affected by several factors. Which of the following is not one of those factors?

   A. Cooking temperature
   B. Speed of heat transfer
   C. Type of thermometer used
   D. Size of the food being cooked

   L.O. 4.3

5. Which of the following cooking methods is best to use to cook delicate food items to doneness without causing them to fall apart?

   A. Poaching
   B. Boiling
   C. Simmering
   D. Blanching

   L.O. 4.5

CHAPTER 5

THE RECIPE: ITS STRUCTURE AND ITS USE

Learning Objectives

After reading this chapter, you should be able to:

5.1   List three basic limitations of written recipes.

5.2   Identify four questions that should be answered when making a recipe for the first time.

5.3   Identify three reasons for using judgment when following a recipe.

5.4   State the two functions of a standardized recipe and list eight types of information it is likely to include.

5.5   Define the purpose of an instructional recipe and describe how it differs from a standardized recipe.

5.6   Identify the three methods used to measure ingredients and provide an example of the types of ingredients commonly measured by each method.

5.7   Name the five techniques used for portion control in plating and service.

5.8   Name the four basic units of measurement in the metric system and what each measures.

5.9   Apply the two-part formula required to convert recipes to a higher or lower yield and identify factors that can negatively impact results when cooking with a converted recipe.

5.10   Define yield-cost analysis and explain the distinction between as purchased and edible portion quantities of food.

5.11   Perform yield cost analysis.

5.12   Calculate raw food costs.

Chapter 5 Study Outline

1. A **standardized recipe** is a set of written instructions for producing a specific dish.

2. When making a recipe for the first time, you should determine the cooking methods used, think about the characteristics and functions of the ingredients, and examine given cooking times.

3. Accurate measurement is critical to the profitability of a restaurant.
   - Measurement by weight is used for most solid ingredients.
     - **As purchased** (AP) weight is the weight before any trimming is done.
     - **Edible portion** (EP) weight is the weight after the item has been washed, trimmed, and prepared in some way.
   - Volume measures are used for most liquids.
   - Dry ingredients are usually weighed in the bakeshop but are often measured by volume in the kitchen for speed.
   - Measurement by count is used when unit sizes are fairly standard or when portion size is based on number of units.

4. **Portion control** ensures that a preparation yields the anticipated number of portions and that each portion is the correct same size.

5. To convert total yield, divide the desired yield by the recipe yield (to get the conversion factor) and then multiply each ingredient quantity by the conversion factor.

6. To change portion size, determine both the total yield of the recipe and the total yield desired, determine the conversion factor (new total yield ÷ old total yield), and then multiply each ingredient by the conversion factor.

7. Every cook should understand yield analysis and food cost percentages.
   - **Food cost percentage** can be calculated as Food cost ÷ Menu price.
   - **Yield tests** are done on meat items to determine costs after all trimming and processing have been done.
   - When portions are based on cooked weight, a **cooked yield test** must be done.

8. **Portion cost** is the total cost of all ingredients in a recipe divided by the number of portions served.

Chapter 5 Exercises

1. Indicate whether each of the following portions is being measured by count (C), weight (W), or volume (V).

    _____(1)   1 scoop ice cream
    _____(2)   2 pear halves
    _____(3)   1 tablespoon olive oil
    _____(4)   1 salmon patty
    _____(5)   6 ounces sliced ham

    _____(6)   250 milligrams pickle relish
    _____(7)   2 slices Swiss cheese
    _____(8)   1 pound cream cheese
    _____(9)   1 cup milk
    _____(10) 2 scoops potato salad

    L.O. 5.6

2. Convert the recipe for Potato Chowder on textbook page 197 so that it yields 4 ½ gallons.
    Potato Chowder

U.S.	Metric	
_____	_____	Salt pork
_____	_____	Onions, medium dice
_____	_____	Celery, medium dice
_____	_____	Flour
_____	_____	Chicken stock
_____	_____	Potatoes, medium dice
_____	_____	Milk, hot
_____	_____	Heavy cream, hot
_____	_____	Salt
_____	_____	White pepper
_____	_____	Chopped parsley

    L.O. 5.9

3. Use the following costs to determine the portion cost for the recipe for Peas à la Française on textbook page 445.

Butter	$2.19/pound
Pearl onions	$2.48/pound
Peas, frozen	$1.79/pound
Lettuce	$14.59/case (12 heads, approx. 2 pounds each)
Parsley	$0.68/oz (approx. 4 tablespoons per ounce)
Salt	$0.65/250 milliliters
Sugar	$0.98/250 milliliters
Chicken stock	$2.39/500 milliliters
Beurre manié	$2.19/pound

a. Total cost _____

b. Portion cost _____

L.O. 5.12

4. List 8 types of information that you are likely to find in a standardized recipe.

- _____
- _____
- _____
- _____
- _____
- _____
- _____
- _____

L.O. 5.4

5. For each of the following categories of measurement, name the basic unit of measure in the metric system and give its standard abbreviation.

_____(1) Weight   _____(3) Length

_____(2) Volume   _____(4) Temperature

L.O. 5.8

6. Name 5 ways of measuring foods when plating to ensure proper portion control.

- _____
- _____
- _____
- _____
- _____

L.O. 5.7

Chapter 5 Check-in

1. In order to determine the EP weight of an item, you need to weigh it

   A. before it is trimmed.
   B. after it has been cooked.
   C. just as it is being served.
   D. after it has been completely trimmed.

   L.O. 5.10

2. Which of the following is an incorrect statement about units of measure in the metric system?

   A. The liter is a measure of volume.
   B. Degree Fahrenheit is a measure of temperature.
   C. The meter is a measure of length.
   D. The basic unit of weight is the gram.

   L.O. 5.8

3. When modifying the yield of a recipe, how do you determine the conversion factor?

   A. Divide the new or desired yield by the old yield.
   B. Divide the old yield by the new or desired yield.
   C. Multiply the new yield by the old yield.
   D. Divide the old yield by the original yield.

   L.O. 5.12

4. Most solid ingredients are measured by

   A. weight.
   B. volume.
   C. count.
   D. standard fill.

   L.O. 5.6

5. Which of the following statements about standardized recipes is not true?

   A. They list exact amounts of ingredients in the order in which they are used.
   B. They indicate cooking times and temperatures.
   C. They do not indicate plating procedures because these are determined by the creativity of the chef.
   D. They are written for specific operations and will indicate specific equipment found in that operation's kitchen.

   L.O. 5.4

CHAPTER 6

THE MENU

Learning Objectives

After reading this chapter, you should be able to:

6.1   Name and explain the factors that influence the make-up of a menu.

6.2   Describe the differences between static and cycle menus, and between *à la carte* and *table d'hôte* menus.

6.3   List in order of their usual service the various courses that might appear in modern menus.

6.4   List three factors that should be considered when creating a balanced menu and provide an example demonstrating the application of each factor.

6.5   Describe three physical conditions that place limitations on menu construction.

6.6   Describe five ways to incorporate the total utilization of foods concept into menu planning.

6.7   List nine ways professional cooks incorporate nutrition principles into their cooking.

Chapter 6 Study Outline

1. A **menu** is a list of dishes served at a meal or available to be served.
2. With few exceptions, the menu must be designed around the tastes and preferences of the target clientele, not the cooks' or managers' choices.
3. Menus vary for different meals.
    *   Breakfast menus feature foods that can be prepared quickly and eaten in a hurry.
    *   Lunch menus should focus on speed, simplicity, and variety.
    *   Dinner is usually eaten leisurely.
4. Types of menus include the following:
    *   **Static**—offers the same dishes every day.
    *   **Cycle**—changes every day for a period and then repeats in the same order.

- **À la carte**—each item listed with its price; customer chooses several to make up a meal.
- **Table d'hôte**—fixed menu with no choices or a selection of complete meals (meal packages) at specified prices.
- **Combination à la carte/table d'hôte**—offers complete meals but with a selection of additional dishes at extra cost.
- **Prix fixe** (fixed price)—menu has only one price for a whole meal; customer chooses one item from each course offering.

5. Many factors go into planning a menu.
   - Courses to include are intended to be eaten at one time.
   - The main dish is the centerpiece of the modern meal.
   - Menus should be balanced with respect to flavor, texture, and appearance.
   - Equipment and personnel, as well as availability of foods, can place limitations on the menu.

6. Total utilization of foods must be planned into menus.
   - All edible trim should be used.
   - Production should be planned to avoid leftovers.
   - "Minimum-use" perishable ingredients should be avoided.

7. Menu items should be labeled accurately with respect to point of origin, grade or quality, cooking method, freshness, whether or not the item is imported or homemade, and size or portion.

8. Those responsible for planning menus need a basic knowledge of nutrition.

9. A **calorie** is the amount of heat needed to raise the temperature of one kilogram of water by 1°C. The body requires calories to live and function.

10. The major nutrients are:
    - Carbohydrates
    - Fats
    - Proteins
    - Vitamins
    - Minerals

11. To stay healthy, people should:
    - Eat a variety of foods.
    - Maintain healthy weight.
    - Choose a diet low in fat and cholesterol, with plenty of vegetables, fruits, and grain products.
    - Consume sugars, salt and sodium, and alcohol in moderation.

12. More and more people are following some form of a vegetarian diet.

13. To prepare more healthful meals:
   - Choose cooking methods that use less fat.
   - Use fresh, high-quality foods, and learn how to enhance natural flavors without salt.
   - Make portion sizes smaller.
   - Hire dietitian services if possible; if not, search out and study some of the many available publications on nutrition.

Chapter 6 Exercises

1. Describe a five-course meal (appetizer, soup, salad, main course, dessert) that balances texture, flavor, and appearance.

   _____

   _____

   _____

L.O. 6.4

2. Match each nutrient on the left with its primary function in the human body on the right.

   _____(1) Carbohydrate
   _____(2) Fat
   _____(3) Protein
   _____(4) Vitamin A
   _____(5) Thiamin
   _____(6) Niacin
   _____(7) Vitamin C
   _____(8) Vitamin E
   _____(9) Calcium
   _____(10) Iron

   a. Promotes healthy bones and teeth
   b. Major building material of all body tissues
   c. Prevents beriberi
   d. Major source of energy
   e. Promotes healing and resistance to infection
   f. Protects other nutrients
   g. Needed to form red blood cells
   h. Supplies essential fatty acids
   i. Promotes healthy nervous system, skin, and digestion
   j. Promotes healthy eyes

L.O. 6.7

3. Match each nutrient on the left with the food on the right in which it is found. Letters will be used more than once, and some might correspond to more than one letter.

_____(1)   Carbohydrate   a.   Oranges
_____(2)   Fat   b.   Whole wheat bread
_____(3)   Protein   c.   Chicken
_____(4)   Vitamin A   d.   Butter
_____(5)   Thiamin
_____(6)   Niacin
_____(7)   Vitamin C
_____(8)   Vitamin E
_____(9)   Calcium
_____(10) Iron

L.O. 6.7

4. Circle the items in the following list that should be eaten only in *moderation* in a healthy diet.

Cheesecake   Brie cheese
Bulgur   Lentils
Grape juice   Tomatoes
Ice cream   Pasta
Canned soups   Cream sauces

L.O. 6.7

5. What are the four primary things chefs and menu planners can do to promote healthy eating?

- _____
- _____
- _____
- _____

L.O. 6.7

6. a. List three types of establishments that are likely to have a cycle menu.

    - _____

    - _____

    - _____

    b. List three types of establishments that are likely to have a static menu.

    - _____

    - _____

    - _____

L.O. 6.2

7. Veal scaloppine is popular in your restaurant. You buy whole legs of veal and cut them yourself into scaloppine. List three ideas for using trimmings from the veal legs to avoid waste.

    - _____

    - _____

    - _____

L.O. 6.6

Chapter 6 Check-in

1. In which of the following establishments would a cycle menu most likely be used?

    A. Off-premise caterer
    B. Quick-service restaurant
    C. Hotel banquet facility
    D. High school cafeteria

    L.O. 6.2

2. If a restaurant is to be successful, the most important factor to consider when planning a menu is

    A. the equipment and physical facilities of the restaurant.
    B. the preferences and demands of the customers.
    C. the skill of the staff.
    D. efficiency of service.

    L.O. 6.1

3. Which of the following is the best description of a calorie?

    A. It indicates the fat content of foods.
    B. It is a measure of the energy value of foods.
    C. It indicates the starch content of foods.
    D. It is a measure of the fat content of food divided by its nutritional value.

    L.O. 6.7

4. Minimum-use ingredients are

    A. supplied by only a few purveyors.
    B. used in only a few items on an establishment's menu.
    C. quickly prepared.
    D. preferred by few chefs.

    L.O. 6.6

5. Which of the following combinations would be an error of balance on a menu?

    A. Acidic or tart food with a fatty food
    B. Combination of colorful vegetables served with roast beef
    C. Clear soup served before a main course with a cream sauce
    D. None of the above are errors.

    L.O. 6.4

CHAPTER 7

Learning Objectives

After reading this chapter, you should be able to:

7.1   Define *mise en place* and explain why care must be taken in its planning.

7.2   Describe the five general steps used in planning *mise en place*.

7.3   Explain the difference in preparation requirements for set meal service and extended meal service.

7.4   List five guidelines to observe when sharpening a chef's knife.

7.5   Demonstrate major cutting techniques required in food preparation.

7.6   Describe basic pre-cooking and marinating procedures.

7.7   Set up and use a standard breading station.

7.8   Define *convenience foods* in the context of *mise en place* and list eight guidelines for their use.

Chapter 7 Study Outline

1. Pre-preparation is crucial to restaurant success because it is only through good organization and timing of tasks that quantity meals can be smoothly served during periods of heavy-volume.
2. *Mise en place* involves having everything in place for the job to be done.
3. The way *mise en place* is done depends in part on the style of meal service.
   - During set meal service, all customers eat at one time.
   - During extended meal service, customers eat at different times.

4. The knife is a basic pre-preparation tool, which is often faster to use and always faster to clean than a cutting machine.
   - The best sharpening tool is a sharpening stone.
   - The steel is used to true the knife edge and maintain its sharpness.
   - Different parts of the blade are appropriate for different purposes, such as slicing, dicing, peeling, chopping, and chiffonade.
5. Blanching or parcooking is done to:
   - increase holding quantities.
   - save time.
   - remove undesirable flavors.
   - enable the product to be processed further.
6. **Marinating** is soaking a food item in a seasoned liquid to flavor and tenderize it.
7. Except for potatoes, most pre-preparation for frying involves breading, dredging with flour, or coating items with batter.
8. Convenience products have been partially or completely prepared or processed.
   - Food workers should know the shelf life of each product, how to defrost frozen foods properly, know how and to what extent the product has been prepared, and how to use proper cooking methods.
   - Convenience products should be handled with care, examined upon receipt, and stored properly.
   - Convenience products are not a substitute for culinary knowledge and skill.

Chapter 7 Exercises

1. Contrast each of the following pairs of terms.

   (1) Set meal service and extended meal service

   _____

   _____

   _____

   (2) A sharpening stone and a steel

   _____

   _____

   _____

   (3) Breading and batter

   _____

   _____

   _____

L.O.7.3, 7.4, 7.7

2. List and briefly illustrate the four main reasons for blanching or parcooking.

   • _____

   • _____

   • _____

   • _____

L.O. 7.6

3. What two things does marinating do for food?

   • _____

   • _____

L.O. 7.6

4. With what substance are foods dredged?

   _____

L.O. 7.7

5. Fill in the following information regarding convenience foods.

a. Definition

_____

b. Two examples

- _____

- _____

c. Three guidelines for handling

- _____

- _____

- _____

L.O. 7.8

6. What are the three stages, in order, of the standard breading procedure?

- _____

- _____

- _____

L.O. 7.7

7. What are the dimensions of the following cuts?

_____(1) Julienne   _____(3) Medium dice

_____(2) Small dice   _____(4) Large dice

L.O. 7.5

Chapter 7 Check-in

1. The term *mise en place* means
   A. advance preparation.
   B. the judgment of the chef.
   C. a menu that is properly planned.
   D. the physical limitations of the kitchen.

   L.O. 7.1

2. Which of the following statements about set meal service is incorrect?
   A. Customers choose menu items from a written menu.
   B. In set meal service, food prepared in large quantities might deteriorate if it is held too long
   C. Small-batch cooking is useful in set meal service to produce fresher food and fewer leftovers.
   D. All customers eat at approximately one time.

   L.O. 7.3

3. What is the function of the steel?
   A. To true the edge of the knife after sharpening
   B. To sharpen knives
   C. To maintain the edge of the knife so that it will stay sharper longer
   D. (A) and (C) are correct.

   L.O. 7.4

4. To cut vegetables into brunoise means to cut them into
   A. large dice.
   B. tiny dice.
   C. fine strips.
   D. French-fry shapes.

   L.O. 7.5

5. In the standard breading procedure, pans are set up in which order?
   A. Crumbs, then eggwash, then flour
   B. Eggwash, then flour, then crumbs
   C. Flour, then eggwash, then crumbs
   D. Flour, then crumbs, then eggwash

   L.O. 7.7

CHAPTER 8

Learning Objectives

After reading this chapter, you should be able to:

8.1   Prepare basic mirepoix.

8.2   Flavor liquids using a sachet or spice bag.

8.3   Prepare white veal or beef stocks, chicken stock, fish stock, and brown stock.

8.4   Cool and store stocks correctly.

8.5   Prepare meat, chicken, and fish glazes.

8.6   Evaluate the quality of convenience bases and use convenience bases.

8.7   Explain the functions of sauces and list five qualities that a sauce adds to foods.

8.8   Prepare white, blonde, and brown roux, and use them to thicken liquids.

8.9   Prepare and use *beurre manie.*

8.10   Thicken liquids with cornstarch and other starches.

8.11   Prepare and use egg yolk and cream liaison.

8.12   Finish a sauce with raw butter (*monter au beurre).*

8.13   Prepare the five leading sauces: Béchamel, Velouté, Brown Sauce or Espagnole, Tomato, and Hollandaise.

8.14   Prepare small sauces from leading sauces.

8.15   Identify and prepare five simple butter sauces.

8.16   Prepare compound butters and list their uses.

8.17   Prepare pan gravies.

Chapter 8 Study Outline

1. Preparing **stock** is a foundational cooking skill.
    - The ingredients for stock are bones, meat, mirepoix, acid products, scraps and leftovers, and seasonings and spices.
    - **Bones** are a source for gelatin to give body to the stock.
    - **Mirepoix** is a combination of celery, carrots, and onions used for flavoring in all areas of cooking.
    - The rule of thumb proportions for ingredients of white, brown, and fish stocks are 50% bones, 10% mirepoix, and 100% water.
2. Blanching bones rids them of some of the impurities that cause cloudiness.
3. **Reduction** is done by boiling or simmering stocks to evaporate part of the water.
4. A **glaze** (glace) is a stock that has been concentrated by reduction until it coats the back of a spoon and is solid and rubbery when refrigerated.
5. A **sauce** is a flavorful liquid, usually thickened, used to flavor, season, and enhance other foods.
6. Sauces incorporate three types of ingredients: a liquid, a thickening agent, and flavoring ingredients.
7. **Roux** is a cooked, stiff mixture of equal parts by weight of flour and fat.
8. Other thickening agents include beurre manié, whitewash, cornstarch, arrowroot, waxy maize, pregelantinized or instant starches, bread crumbs, vegetable purées, and ground nuts.
9. Finishing techniques include reduction, straining, deglazing, enriching, and seasoning.
10. Leading sauces are:
    - Béchamel
    - Velouté
    - Brown
    - Tomato
    - Hollandaise

Chapter 8 Exercises

1. What is the difference between white stocks and brown stocks?

    _____

    _____

L.O. 8.3

2. Why are bones sometimes blanched before being used in a stock?

_____

_____

L.O. 8.3

3. Name the ingredients used when making each of the following items.
   (1) Stock

   _____

   _____

   (2) Roux

   _____

   _____

L.O. 8.3, 8.8

4. Match each cooking term on the left with its description on the right.

   _____(1) Deglazing   a. Thickening by removing liquid
   _____(2) Enriching   b. Creating extra smoothness before
   _____(3) Reduction   final seasoning
   _____(4) Seasoning   c. Removing and dissolving cooked
   _____(5) Straining   food particles from the bottom of
                                   the pan
                               d. Adding butter to give extra flavor
                                   and shine
                               e. Adding ingredients such as salt at
                                   the end of cooking

L.O. 8.14

5. Match each sauce on the left with the leading sauce on the right from which it is derived.

   _____(1) Lyonnaise   a. Béchamel
   _____(2) Mousseline   b. Veal velouté
   _____(3) Mushroom   c. Chicken velouté
                               d. Fish velouté
   _____(4) Aurora   e. Espagnole
   _____(5) Creole   f. Tomato
   _____(6) Mornay   g. Hollandaise
   _____(7) Bercy

L.O. 8.14

42

6. Match each leading sauce on the left with its primary ingredients on the right.

_____(1) Béchamel

_____(2) Velouté

_____(3) Brown

_____(4) Tomato

_____(5) Hollandaise

a. Mirepoix, roux, brown stock, tomato purée, herbs

b. Roux and veal, chicken, or fish stock

c. Roux, milk, onion, herbs, spices

d. Butter, egg yolks, lemon juice, cayenne

e. Salt pork, onion, carrots, tomatoes, ham bones, herbs

L.O. 8.13

Chapter 8 Check-in

1. Some of the herbs and spices most frequently used in a sachet for making stocks are

   A. thyme, parsley, and bay leaf.
   B. parsley, basil, and tarragon.
   C. thyme, tarragon, and bay leaf.
   D. sage, cloves, and peppercorns.

   L.O. 8.2

2. How long should veal stock be simmered?

   A. 1 to2 hour
   B. 3 to 4 hours
   C. 6 to 8 hours
   D. 12 to 14 hours

   L.O. 8.3

3. What is the name of the procedure for making meat glaze from brown stock?

   A. Reduction
   B. Deglazing
   C. Tempering
   D. Straining

   L.O. 8.5

4. What is the proper time for adding a liaison to a sauce?

   A. At the end, just before the sauce is served
   B. At the beginning
   C. While the sauce is being reduced
   D. Just before the sauce is reduced

   L.O. 8.11

5. Which of the following thickening agents is made with the same ingredients as roux?

   A. Liaison
   B. Whitewash
   C. Slurry
   D. Beurre manié

   L.O. 8.8, 8.9

CHAPTER 9

Learning Objectives

After reading this chapter, you should be able to:

9.1 Describe three basic categories of soups.

9.2 Identify standard appetizer and main course portion sizes for soups.

9.3 State the procedures for holding soups for service and for serving soups at the proper temperatures.

9.4 List three groups of soup garnishes.

9.5 Prepare clarified consommé.

9.6 Prepare vegetable soups and other clear soups.

9.7 Prepare cream soups.

9.8 Prepare purée soups.

9.9 Prepare bisques, chowders, specialty soups, and national soups.

Chapter 9 Study Outline

1. There are three basic types of soups.
   - Clear, unthickened types include **broth** and **bouillon**, **vegetable**, and **consommé**.
   - Thickened soups are opaque and include **cream soups**, **purées**, **bisques**, **chowders**, and **potage**.
   - Specialty and national soups that do not fit into the main categories include those requiring unusual ingredients or preparation methods, as well as some cold soups.
   - Many vegetable-based soups are suitable for vegetarian menus.
2. Rich, strong flavor is most important to consommé, with clarity being second in importance.
3. The mixture of ingredients used to clarify a stock is called the **clearmeat** or the **clarification** and includes lean ground meat, egg whites, mirepoix, and acid ingredients.
4. The basic technique for producing cream soups is dilution and flavoring of Velouté or Béchamel sauces.

- Roux and other starch thickeners stabilize milk products and prevent curdling.
- Cream soups should have the consistency of heavy cream, a smooth texture, and the flavor of their main ingredients.

5. Puréed soups are made by simmering fresh or dried vegetables in water or stock and then puréeing the soup.

6. A bisque is a cream soup made with shellfish.

7. Chowders are chunky, hearty soups, most of which are based on fish, shellfish, or vegetables, and contain potatoes and milk or cream.

Chapter 9 Exercises

1. How would each of the following soups be classified?

_____(1) Turtle soup

_____(2) Split pea soup

_____(3) Bouillon

_____(4) Consommé

_____(5) Cream of mushroom soup

_____(6) Navy bean soup

_____(7) Scotch broth

_____(8) Chicken noodle soup

_____(9) Shrimp bisque

_____(10) Oxtail soup

L.O. 9.1

2. a. When used correctly, what does clearmeat do in consommé?

_____

_____

   b. What are the ingredients of clearmeat?

_____

_____

L.O. 9.5

3. Match each garnished consommé with its lettered garnish ingredient.

_____(1) Consommé Brunoise

_____(2) Consommé Julienne

_____(3) Consommé Printanière

_____(4) Consommé Paysanne

_____(5) Consommé Vermicelli

a. Onion or leek, carrot, celery, and turnip, cut into long, slightly thick strips

b. Diced spring vegetables

c. Cooked thin spaghetti

d. Thin slices of leeks, carrots, celery, turnip, and cabbage

e. Onion or leek, carrot, celery, and turnip, cut into long, thin strips

L.O. 9.5

4. The combination of which two types of ingredients will cause a soup to curdle?

• _____

• _____

L.O. 9.7

5. Describe the thickness, texture, and taste of a good-quality cream soup.

(1) Thickness

_____

_____

(2) Texture

_____

_____

(3) Taste

_____

_____

L.O. 9.7

6. Match each numbered soup with its lettered description.

_____(1) Chowder

_____(2) Borscht

_____(3) Minestrone

_____(4) Gazpacho

a. Tomato-broth vegetable soup

b. Cold tomatoes, cucumbers, onions, green peppers, and garlic

c. Beet soup

d. Chunky soup usually containing milk and potatoes

L.O. 9.9

7. a. Approximately how many appetizer portions can you get out of one gallon of soup?

    _____

    b. How many main-course portion sizes can you get out of one gallon of soup?

    _____

L.O. 9.2

8. In terms of the thickening agents used, what is the difference between cream soups and purée soups?

    _____

    _____

    _____

L.O. 9.7, 9.8

Chapter 9 Check-in

1. Which of the following is not a basic category of soup?

    A. Thin soups
    B. Thick soups
    C. Clear soups
    D. Specialty and national soups

    L.O. 9.1

2. Standard metric portion size for soup as an appetizer is

    A. 300–350 milliliters
    B. 440–500 milliliters
    C. 125–150 milliliters
    D. 200–250 milliliters

    L.O. 9.2

3. You are likely to see the word "raft" in a recipe for

    A. clam chowder.
    B. chicken noodle soup.
    C. beef consommé.
    D. shrimp bisque.

    L.O. 9.5

4. When you are making a clear vegetable soup, it is a good practice to

    A. add all vegetables at the same time so that they are evenly cooked.
    B. cook vegetables slowly in a little butter before adding stock, to give them a richer, mellower taste.
    C. cook starchy products along with the other vegetables so that the flavors will blend.
    D. use as many vegetables as possible.

    L.O. 9.6

5. Which of the following is not one of the three basic types of soup garnish?

    A. Solid garnish
    B. Garnish in the soup
    C. Toppings
    D. Accompaniments

    L.O. 9.4

CHAPTER 10

UNDERSTANDING MEATS AND GAME

Learning Objectives

After reading this chapter, you should be able to:

10.1   Describe the composition and structure of meat and explain how they relate to meat selection and cooking methods.

10.2   Explain the use of the federal meat inspection and grading system in selecting and purchasing meats.

10.3   Explain the effect that aging has on meat and identify the two primary aging methods.

10.4   Identify the primal cuts of beef, lamb, veal, and pork, and list the major fabricated cuts obtained from each of them.

10.5   Choose appropriate cooking methods for the most important meat cuts, based on the meat's tenderness and other characteristics.

10.6   Prepare variety meats.

10.7   Identify the characteristics of game meats and select the appropriate cooking methods for them.

10.8   Determine doneness in cooked meat.

10.9   Store fresh meat and frozen meat to gain the maximum shelf life.

Chapter 10 Study Outline

1. Muscle tissue is composed of water, protein, fat, and a very small amount of carbohydrate.

2. Lean meat is composed of long, thin muscle fibers bound together in a network of proteins called **connective tissue.**

   - Meats highest in connective tissue come from exercised muscles or older animals.

   - The two kinds of connective tissue are **collagen** and **elastin.**

3. All meat must undergo federal inspection, which guarantees wholesomeness.

4. **Aging** meat before cooking is the process of holding newly-slaughtered (green) carcasses in coolers to provide time for natural enzymes to soften tissues.

5. Cuts are based on muscle and bone structure and the various parts' uses and cooking methods.

   - Carcasses (the whole animal) are seldom used by foodservice operations.

   - Sides, quarters, foresaddles, and hindsaddles also are not frequently used in food service.

   - Primal or wholesale cuts are small enough for use in some restaurant kitchens.

   - Fabricated (small) cuts, including portion control cuts, are the most expensive per pound but require the least amount of labor.

6. The Institution Meat Purchase Specifications (IMPS) and National Association of Meat Purveyors Specifications (NAMPS) systems allow purchasers to order exactly the kind of cuts they need from packers who use these systems.

7. In general, most meat cooking methods should use low temperatures because high heat toughens, dries, and shrinks meats.

8. Meats high in fat are usually cooked without added fat; those low in fat can be **barded** or **larded** to prevent dryness.

9. Factors influencing choice of cooking method include developing tenderness and flavor, preventing excessive shrinkage and nutrient loss, and developing appearance.

10. Doneness and ways to judge it vary depending on the cooking method used.

    - Pork is probably best cooked to between 160°F–170°F (71.1°C–76.7°C) to guard against trichinosis but to avoid drying.

    - Testing the interior of meat with a meat thermometer is the most accurate method of testing doneness.

    - To account for carry-over cooking, remove a roast from the oven when the thermometer reads 10°F–15°F (-12.2°C – -9.4°C) below the target reading and let it stand 15 to 30 minutes before slicing.

11. Variety meats include liver, kidneys, sweetbreads, brains, heart, tongue, tripe, and oxtails.
12. Fresh meat is highly perishable and should be stored properly to prevent spoilage.

Chapter 10 Exercises

1. What is the difference between collagen and elastin?

_____

_____

L.O. 10.1

2. You are the owner-chef of The Great American Grill, a 75-seat restaurant with a mixed menu that includes meat and poultry items. You have one full-time person on staff for cooking and preparation assistance. Your cold and dry storage space is somewhat limited. You have a freezer but not a walk-in cooler. What market forms of meat are you likely to order most frequently? Why?

_____

_____

_____

_____

_____

L.O. 10.4

3. a. What happens to meat when it is aged under controlled temperatures?

_____

_____

   b. What is "green" meat?

_____

_____

   c. What is the difference between wet aging and dry aging?

_____

_____

L.O. 10.3

4. Indicate whether each beef cut below is better suited to a dry-heat (D) or a moist-heat (M) cooking method.

_____(1) Chuck

_____(2) Shank

_____(3) Rib (roast)

_____(4) Sirloin

_____(5) Flank

_____(6) Round

L.O. 10.5

5. Describe the color of rare, medium, and well-done meats and explain how they feel.

(1) Rare

_____

_____

(2) Medium

_____

_____

(3) Well-done

_____

_____

L.O. 10.8

6. What are variety meats?

_____

_____

_____

L.O. 10.6

Chapter 10 Check-in

1. About 75% of muscle tissue, or meat, is

   A. protein.
   B. water.
   C. fat.
   D. collagen.

   L.O. 10.1

2. What does a federal inspection mean when stamped on a meat carcass?

   A. The meat has a good ratio of lean to fat.
   B. The meat is tender and of a high grade.
   C. The meat is wholesome and fit to eat.
   D. The meat has been properly aged.

   L.O. 10.2

3. What is the most accurate way to test the doneness of a large roast?

   A. Press on the meat with the fingertips. The meat's firmness indicates doneness.
   B. Pierce the meat and observe the color of the juices that run out.
   C. Use a meat thermometer to test the internal temperature.
   D. Calculate the proper cooking time using an accurate meat roasting chart.

   L.O. 10.8

4. What does the term "green" mean when applied to meat?

   A. The meat has not been properly aged/
   B. The meat is moldy.
   C. The meat is packed and aged in a vacuum pack.
   D. The meat is dry-aged.

   L.O. 10.3

5. Which of the following beef cuts comes from the forequarter?

   A. Sirloin
   B. Brisket
   C. Flank
   D. Top round

   L.O. 10.4

CHAPTER 11

Learning Objectives

After reading this chapter, you should be able to:

11.1   Cook meats by roasting and baking.

11.2   Cook meats by broiling, grilling, and pan-broiling.

11.3   Cook meats by sautéing, pan-frying, and griddling.

11.4   Cook meats by simmering.

11.5   Cook meats by braising.

11.6   Cook variety meats.

Chapter 11 Study Outline

1. Continuous low-temperature roasting produces the best product, with the range 250°F to 325°F (121.1°C to 163°C), depending on the size of the cut and the production schedule.

   - Small pieces of meat can be successfully roasted to the rare stage at high temperatures.

   - Convection ovens work well for browning and high-temperature roasting but can dry out large roasts.

   - Most chefs believe that meats are best roasted fat side up.

2. The goal of the dry-heat methods—broiling, grilling, and pan-broiling—is to achieve the desired amount of browning doneness.

   - The shorter the cooking time, the higher the temperature.

   - Cooking time depends on the desired doneness and the thickness of the cut.

3. Sautéing, pan-frying, and griddling differ by the amount of fat used.

   - Sautéing uses high heat and a small amount of fat and is usually used for small pieces of food.

   - Pan-frying uses moderate heat, a moderate amount of fat, and is usually used with larger items.

   - A sauce made by deglazing the pan often accompanies sautéed meats.

4. Simmering is appropriate for tougher cuts of meat.

- **Stewing** means cooking small pieces of meat by simmering or by braising.
- Stews are served in a sauce or gravy made of the cooking liquid.
5. Braising is a combination of dry-heat and moist-heat cooking methods.
    - Meats are first browned or seared and then simmered.
    - Meat quality depends on the quality of the stock in which the item is cooked.

Chapter 11 Exercises

1. Describe how meat is seared as part of the roasting method.

_____

_____

_____

L.O. 11.1

2. Which meat cooking method(s):
    (1) Can produce line marks on meat?

    _____

    (2) Can be used to prepare shish kebabs?

    _____

    (3) Can be used to prepare rack of lamb?

    _____

    (4) Is a combination of dry heat and moist heat?

    _____

    (5) Is often used with cured products such as corned beef?

    _____

    (6) Presents the problem of keeping meats juicy in the well-done stage because of the extremely high cooking temperatures?

    _____

    (7) Is not frequently used for meats?

    _____

    (8) Cooks the meat and produces a sauce at the same time?

    _____

L.O. 11.1–11.5

3. What is the difference between sautéing and pan-frying?

_____

_____

_____

L.O. 11.3

4. In one method of braising meats, the meat is cooked in a flavorful stock, and the stock is made into a sauce after the meat is cooked. The steps for this method are out of order below. Put them in correct order, writing the number 1 before the first step, number 2 before the second step, etc.

_____Skim fat from braising liquid. Make a roux and thicken braising liquid with it.

_____Add mirepoix and brown it in the fat left in the pan.

_____Strain and adjust seasonings of sauce.

_____Collect all equipment and food supplies.

_____Put meat in pan and brown it well on all sides.

_____Serve meat with the sauce.

_____Heat a small amount of fat in the braising pan.

_____Replace meat in pan; add stock or other braising liquid, tomato product, and sachet.

_____Trim and prepare meat for cooking as required.

_____Take cooked meat out of the braising liquid and keep the meat warm.

_____Simmer with cover on until the meat is tender.

L.O. 11.5

5. When using a standard thermometer (not an instant-read thermometer) for roasting meats, how should the tip of the thermometer be positioned in the meat?

_____

_____

L.O. 11.1

6. What is the main purpose of using mirepoix when roasting meats?

_____

_____

_____

L.O. 11.1

Chapter 11 Check-in

1. Which of the following cuts would you most likely roast at a high temperature?

    A. 30-pound (14-kilogram) steamship round of beef
    B. 2-pound (900 gram) beef tenderloin section, roasted rare
    C. 6-pound (2.7 kilogram) pork loin, well done
    D. 7-pound (3.2 kilogram) leg of lamb, medium done

    L.O. 11.1

2. Which of the following should not be cooked by sautéing?

    A. Slices of leg of veal
    B. Pork tenderloin, cut into slices
    C. Medallions of lamb loin
    D. Slices of lamb shank

    L.O. 11.3

3. A blanquette is a

    A. brown stew.
    B. white stew cooked by braising.
    C. white stew cooked by simmering.
    D. braised dish flavored with curry.

    L.O. 11.4

4. Which of the following statements is true?

    A. Broiling uses lower heat than sautéing.
    B. Broiling is a moist-heat cooking method.
    C. Broiling is a good cooking method for less-tender cuts of meat.
    D. Broiled meats are best cooked to the rare or medium stage.

    L.O. 11.2

5. Which of the following is a good practice when browning meat as part of the braising procedure?

    A. Dry the meat before browning it.
    B. Salt the meat before browning so that the salt will be absorbed into the meat.
    C. Do not marinate meat that is to be browned because the marinade will make it difficult to brown the meat.
    D. Make sure the meat is moist before browning so that it does not dry out.

    L.O. 11.5

CHAPTER 12

UNDERSTANDING POULTRY AND GAME BIRDS

Learning Objectives

After reading this chapter, you should be able to:

12.1   Explain the differences between light meat and dark meat, and describe how these differences affect cooking.

12.2   Describe four techniques that help keep chicken or turkey breast moist while roasting.

12.3   Define the following terms used to classify poultry: *kind*, *class*, and *style*.

12.4   Identify popular types of farm-raised game birds and the cooking methods appropriate to their preparation.

12.5   Store poultry items.

12.6   Determine doneness in cooked poultry, both large roasted birds and smaller birds.

12.7   Truss poultry for cooking.

12.8   Cut chicken into parts.

Chapter 12 Study Outline

1. Most poultry has less fat than animal meats and is too young to have developed much tough connective tissue.

2. Older birds need moist-heat cooking to tenderize them.

3. Free-range chickens, allowed to move around freely and eat outdoors, are expensive. Some people feel that they are more flavorful and worth the extra cost.

4. Chicken and turkey consist of two parts.

    • The breast and wings are "light meat" and cook faster.

    • The legs are "dark meat" and take longer to cook.

    • Duck and goose have all dark meat.

5. A major problem in roasting poultry whole is cooking the legs to doneness without overcooking the breast. Solutions to the problem include:

- Roasting breast down for part of the cooking time.
- Basting with fat only.
- Barding the bird.
- Separating breast from leg sections and roasting each for a different amount of time.

6. Poultry is classified by kind, class, and style.
   - Chicken is most commonly used.
   - Turkeys are larger birds that are usually roasted.
   - Ducks and geese are also usually roasted.
   - Guineas are a domestically raised descendent of the pheasant.
   - Squabs are young, domestically raised pigeons.

7. Guidelines for poultry handling, storage, and doneness include:
   - Fresh birds should be transported and stored on ice until use, preferably within 24 hours, and should be handled properly to avoid potential salmonella cross-contamination.
   - Frozen poultry should be thawed in the refrigerator, and thawed birds should not be refrozen.
   - Poultry is always cooked well-done.
     - Test large birds by inserting a thermometer into the thickest part of the thigh.
     - When done, small birds are firm, with loose joints and flesh separating from the bone, and their juices are clear.

8. **Trussing** ensures even cooking and attractive appearance.

Chapter 12 Exercises

1. Indicate whether each of the following chicken or turkey parts is considered light (L) or dark (D) meat.
   _____(1)Thigh
   _____(2)Wing
   _____(3)Breast
   _____(4)Drumstick

L.O. 12.1

2. What is a major problem in cooking poultry whole?

_____

_____

_____

L.O. 12.1, 12.2

3. What does it mean to truss poultry? Why is it done?

_____

_____

_____

L.O. 12.7

4. How does the age of the bird affect poultry?

_____

_____

_____

L.O. 12.3

5. Rank the following chickens in order from youngest (1) to oldest (5).
    _____Rock Cornish game hen
    _____Broiler (fryer)
    _____Cock (rooster)
    _____Capon
    _____Roaster
L.O. 12.3

6. Rank the following from the smallest (1) to the largest (5)
    _____Partridge
    _____Pheasant
    _____Duckling
    _____Quail
    _____Goose
L.O. 12.3, 12.4

60

Chapter 13 Check-in

1. Recommended roasting temperature for a large turkey is
   A. 375–400°F (190–200°C) until starting to brown, then 300°F (150°C) until done.
   B. 300°F (150°C) until nearly done, then 375–400°F (190–200°C) until done.
   C. 300°F (150°C) until done.
   D. 375°F (190°C) until done.

   L.O. 13.1

2. Which of the following types of chickens is best for deep-frying?
   A. Fowl
   B. Capon
   C. Cock or rooster
   D. Broiler

   L.O. 13.3

3. A chicken fricassee is a
   A. white stew cooked by braising.
   B. curried chicken dish cooked by simmering.
   C. type of broiled chicken flavored with mustard.
   D. chicken braised with mushrooms, tomato, and parsley.

   L.O. 13.5

4. How does the broiling temperature for chicken compare with the broiling temperature for lamb chops?
   A. Chicken is broiled at the same temperature as lamb chops.
   B. Chicken is broiled at a higher temperature.
   C. Chicken is broiled at a lower temperature.
   D. Chicken is started at a higher temperature than lamb chops, and after the chicken is brown the temperature is lowered so that it is about the same as for lamb chops.

   L.O. 13.2

5. If you wanted to make a dish of poached chicken, the best part of the chicken to select is the
   A. Thigh
   B. Wing
   C. Drumstick
   D. Breast

   L.O. 13.4

CHAPTER 14

UNDERSTANDING FISH AND SHELLFISH

Learning Objectives

After reading this chapter, you should be able to:

14.1   Explain how the cooking qualities of fish are affected by the lack of connective tissue.

14.2   Determine doneness in cooked fish.

14.3   Demonstrate the appropriate cooking methods for fat and lean fish.

14.4   List seven basic market forms of fish.

14.5   Dress and fillet round fish and flatfish.

14.6   List and describe common varieties of saltwater and freshwater fin fish used in American food service.

14.7   Identify the characteristics of fresh fish, and contrast them with characteristics of not-so-fresh fish.

14.8   Store fish and fish products.

14.9   Identify the popular varieties of shellfish and discuss their characteristics.

14.10 Outline the special safe handling and cooking procedures for shellfish.

14.11 Open clams and oysters, split lobster, and peel and devein shrimp.

Chapter 14 Study Outline

1. Fish flesh has the same general composition as that of poultry and meat, but it is naturally tender and quick to cook because it has little connective tissue. Any toughening is due to high heat, not connective tissue.

2. Fish is delicate and easily overcooked.
   - It is done when the flesh just begins to flake into natural separations, separates from the bone, and has changed from translucent to opaque.
   - Which moist-heat, dry-heat, or dry-heat with fat method is best depends on the size of the fish and its fat content.

3. Fish are available in several forms or may be cut by the cook.
   - Most operations buy fish in the forms in which they intend to cook them, but others buy whole fish.

4. There are hundreds of varieties of fish, but relatively few species account for the majority used in American food service.
   - Flatfish have lean, white flesh; a mild, delicate flavor; an oval, flat body; and both eyes on one side of the head.
   - Saltwater fish are either flatfish or round fish.
   - Freshwater fish include catfish, perch, pike, tilapia, trout, and whitefish.

5. Fresh fish are extremely perishable and are not federally inspected. They should be stored on crushed ice if possible (whole or drawn fish unwrapped and cut fish wrapped) or (all forms wrapped) refrigerated at 30°F to 34°F (−1.1°C to 1.1°C) and used within a day or two.

6. Some processed fish products are inspected and graded under a voluntary federal system.

7. Thaw in the refrigerator or, if necessary, under cold running water, or cook small pieces without thawing; do not refreeze.

8. **Mollusks** are soft animals with hard shells and no internal skeleton. They include oysters, clams, scallops, squid, and octopus.

9. **Crustaceans** have segmented shells and jointed legs. Those used frequently in commercial kitchens are lobsters, rock lobsters, shrimp, and crabs.

10. Other seafood items that play a role in food service are snails (escargot), frogs (frogs' legs), and surimi (a processed seafood product made from lean, inexpensive white fish).

Chapter 14 Exercises

1. How is the flesh of fish different from the flesh of meat and poultry?

    _____

    _____

    _____

L.O. 14.1

2. Indicate whether each of the following fish is flat (F) or round (R).

    _____(1)   Sole   _____(6)   Salmon
    _____(2)   Grouper   _____(7)   Shad
    _____(3)   Bluefish   _____(8)   Halibut
    _____(4)   Turbot   _____(9)   Tilefish
    _____(5)   Red snapper   _____(10)   Flounder

L.O. 14.6

3. Indicate whether each of the following fish is saltwater (S) or freshwater (F).

    _____(1)   Cod   _____(6)   Catfish
    _____(2)   Pompano   _____(7)   Whiting
    _____(3)   Perch   _____(8)   Mackerel
    _____(4)   Tuna   _____(9)   Halibut
    _____(5)   Trout   _____(10)   Tilapia

L.O. 14.6

4. Indicate whether each of the following fish is fat (F) or lean (L).

    _____(1)   Bluefish   _____(6)   Swordfish
    _____(2)   Shad   _____(7)   Perch
    _____(3)   Salmon   _____(8)   Haddock
    _____(4)   Whitefish   _____(9)   Jack
    _____(5)   Whiting   _____(10)   Mahi-mahi

L.O. 14.3, 14.6

5. Identify five qualities of fresh fish.

  - _____
  - _____
  - _____
  - _____
  - _____

L.O. 14.7

6. a. What is the difference between a mollusk and a crustacean?

  _____
  _____
  _____

  b. Provide three examples of each that are commonly used in commercial kitchens.

  - _____   - _____
  - _____   - _____
  - _____   - _____

L.O. 14.9

7. Identify the native region or location of each of the following crab varieties.

  _____(1) Dungeness   _____(4) Blue
  _____(2) Soft-shell   _____(5) Stone
  _____(3) King   _____(6) Snow

L.O. 14.9

8. What is the best way to store fresh clams and oysters in the shell?

  _____
  _____
  _____

L.O. 14.8, 14.10

9. What is the best way to store whole fin fish?

_____

_____

_____

Chapter 14 Check-in

1. One of the most important differences between fish and meat is that fish

   A. cooks more slowly.
   B. is naturally much tougher.
   C. has less connective tissue.
   D. must be cooked with moist-heat methods to be made tender.

   L.O. 14.1

2. Which of the following is considered a lean fish?

   A. Tuna
   B. Mackerel
   C. Sole
   D. Salmon

   L.O. 14.3, 14.6

3. Which of the following is a good sign of proper doneness in fish?

   A. The flesh falls apart easily.
   B. The bones turn from white to pink.
   C. The eyes turn opaque.
   D. The flesh turns from translucent to opaque.

   L.O. 14.2

4. Three of the following are good indications of the freshness of fish. Which one is not?

   A. The gills are gray or brown.
   B. The aroma of the fish is mild.
   C. The fish's eyes are clear and bulging.
   D. The flesh is firm.

   L.O. 14.7

5. A sea animal with jointed legs and a segmented shell is called a

   A. cephalopod.
   B. mollusk.
   C. crustacean.
   D. tomalley.

   L.O. 14.9

CHAPTER 15

COOKING FISH AND SHELLFISH

Learning Objectives

After reading this chapter, you should be able to:

15.1   Cook fish and shellfish by baking.

15.2   Cook fish and shellfish by broiling.

15.3   Cook fish and shellfish by sautéing and pan-frying.

15.4   Cook fish and shellfish by deep-frying.

15.5   Cook fish and shellfish by poaching in court bouillon.

15.6   Cook fish and shellfish by poaching in fumet and wine.

15.7   Cook fish and shellfish by mixed cooking techniques.

15.8   Prepare dishes made of raw seafood.

Chapter 15 Study Outline

1. When baking fish and shellfish, avoid overcooking.
   - Fat fish are best for baking.
   - At 400°F, fish should be baked about ten minutes per inch of thickness.
   - Baking fish with moist ingredients or with liquids is called braising.

2. Fish and seafood to be broiled are often coated with fat, dredged, and turned during cooking.

3. A classic method of sautéing fish, **à la meunière** requires dredging the product in flour and then sautéing it in clarified butter or oil. It is then sprinkled with lemon juice, parsley, and hot brown butter.

4. Lean fish are especially well suited to sautéing.

5. Deep-frying is probably the most popular way to prepare fish in North America.
   - Fish to be fried is breaded or battered.
   - Frozen breaded fish should be fried without thawing.

6. Whole fish and thick steaks may be cooked in **court bouillon,** a quickly-made mixture of water, an acid ingredient, herbs, and seasonings.

7. Poaching fish in white wine and fumet produces a delicate flavor.

Chapter 15 Exercises

1. How does the procedure for braising fish differ from the procedure for baking fish?

   _____

   _____

   _____

L.O. 15.1

2. What should be done to rock lobster before broiling to prevent dryness?

   _____

   _____

   _____

L.O. 15.2

3. Describe each of the following:
   (1) Fish à la meunière

   _____

   (2) Court bouillon

   _____

   (3) Cooking en papillote

   _____

   (4) Fish tartar

   _____

L.O. 15.3, 15.5, 15.7, 15.8

4. Which cooking method is used to prepare each of the following?
    (1) Marinated fillets of red snapper

    _____

    (2) Crab cakes with roasted pepper rémoulade

    _____

    (3) Fillets of sole meunière

    _____

    (4) Sole vin blanc

    _____

    (5) Oysters casino

    _____

    (6) Smoke-roasted salmon fillet with pepper salad

    _____

    (7) Escalope of salmon with sorrel

    _____

L.O. 15.1–15.7

5. The breading on deep-fried fish serves several purposes. List three of these purposes.
    *   _____
    *   _____
    *   _____

L.O. 15.4

6. The following are the steps in the procedure for poaching fish in fumet and wine, but every other step has been left out. Fill in the blanks with the missing steps.

- Collect all equipment and food supplies.
- _____

- Arrange the fish portions in the pan in a single layer. Season them lightly.
- _____

- Cover the fish with a piece of buttered parchment or other paper and cover the pan with a lid.
- _____

- Drain the liquid into a wide pan. Keep the fish warm.
- _____

- Add fish velouté and heavy cream. Bring to a simmer and season with salt, white pepper, and lemon juice. If desired, finish the sauce with raw butter or a liaison.
- _____

- Plate the fish and coat with the sauce.
- _____

L.O. 15.6

Chapter 15 Check-in

1. To prepare fish à la meunière, which of the following ingredients will you not need?

   A. Cornmeal
   B. Lemon juice
   C. Butter
   D. Parsley

   L.O. 15.3

2. To apply the standard breading procedure to fish fillets, pans should be set up in which order?

   A. Crumbs, then eggwash, then flour
   B. Eggwash, then flour, then crumbs
   C. Flour, then eggwash, then crumbs
   D. Flour, then crumbs, then eggwash

   L.O. 15.4

3. Which of the following is not a good guideline for broiling fish?

   A. Fat fish is best for broiling, as it is less likely to dry out.
   B. Skin should always be removed from fillets before broiling, as it will split and mar the appearance.
   C. Coat the fish lightly with fat before broiling.
   D. Thin fillets can be arranged on a sheet pan and broiled without turning over.

   L.O. 15.2

4. Fish fillets to be baked on a dry sheet pan should be lightly coated with fat

   A. on the top.
   B. on the bottom.
   C. on the top and bottom.
   D. neither. They should be brushed with fat after baking.

   L.O. 15.1

5. Which of the following is not a normal ingredient in a court bouillon?

   A. An acid ingredient, such as lemon juice
   B. Water
   C. Milk
   D. tomato product

   L.O. 15.5

CHAPTER 16

UNDERSTANDING VEGETABLES

Learning Objectives

After reading this chapter, you should be able to:

16.1   Describe the factors that influence texture, flavor, color, and nutritional changes when cooking vegetables.

16.2   Cook vegetables to their proper doneness.

16.3   Judge quality in cooked vegetables based on color, appearance, texture, flavor, seasonings, and appropriateness of combination with sauces or other vegetables.

16.4   Perform the pre-preparation tasks for fresh vegetables.

16.5   Calculate yields based on trimming losses.

16.6   Determine the quality of frozen and canned vegetables.

16.7   Prepare vegetables using the batch cooking method and the blanch and chill method.

16.8   Store both fresh and processed vegetables.

Chapter 16 Study Outline

1. Modern vegetable cooking methods are aimed at preserving and enhancing vegetables' most appealing quality—freshness—by controlling changes in flavor, color, texture, and nutrients during cooking.

    *   Texture depends mostly on the amount of starch and fiber in the vegetable.
    *   Flavor loss is related to length of cooking and, in some cases, the amount of water used.
    *   Acids and alkalis dull or brighten white, red, green, and yellow vegetable pigments and affect choice of cooking methods.
    *   Nutrients can be lost during cooking due to high temperatures, long cooking, leaching, alkalis, or oxygen destruction of plant enzymes.

2. Among the general rules of vegetable cookery are:
   - Do not overcook.
   - Cook as close to service time as possible.
   - If cooked ahead, undercook slightly.
   - Do not use baking soda with green vegetables.
   - Cut vegetables uniformly.
   - Start with boiling salted water.
   - Cook green vegetables and strongly flavored vegetables uncovered.
   - Cook red and white vegetables in slightly acidic liquid to preserve color.
   - Do not mix batches of cooked vegetables.
3. Fresh vegetables should be washed and drained thoroughly, peeled as thinly as possible, and cut into uniform pieces.
4. The cook must know how much of a vegetable's **AP weight** is left after pre-preparation to produce the ready-to-cook item, or **EP weight**.
   - To calculate yield, multiply the percentage yield by the AP weight.
   - To calculate amount needed, divide the EP weight needed by the percentage yield.
5. Although canned or frozen vegetables are not as desirable as good-quality fresh ones, foodservice organizations necessarily use a large quantity of processed vegetables.
   - When handling frozen processed vegetables, check frozen products for quality and cook frozen items from the frozen state.
   - When handling canned vegetables, reject damaged cans, know the drained weight, and check the grade.
6. The two kinds of dried vegetables are legumes and freeze-dried vegetables.
7. Batch cooking, blanching vegetables, and holding them chilled will maintain their quality in quantity cooking.

Chapter 16 Exercises

1. Name five ingredients that will make vegetable fibers firmer, requiring longer cooking times.
   - _____
   - _____
   - _____
   - _____
   - _____

L.O. 16.1

2. Name two things that will soften vegetable fibers.

- _____

- _____

L.O. 16.2

3. How should each of the following vegetables be prepared before cooking?

   (1) Corn (on the cob)

   _____

   _____

   (2) Carrots

   _____

   _____

   (3) Dry onions

   _____

   _____

L.O. 16.4

4. Name four things that are harmful to vegetables' nutrients.

- _____

- _____

- _____

- _____

L.O. 16.1

5. Describe the standards of quality for steamed broccoli regarding the following characteristics.

   (1) Color

   _____

   _____

   (2) Appearance

   _____

   _____

   (3) Texture

   _____

   _____

   (4) Flavor

   _____

   _____

L.O. 16.3

6. Using Table 16.2 on text page 437, determine the amount that each of the following AP amounts will yield.

   _____8 pounds of asparagus

   _____4 pounds of green beans

   _____12 pounds of cabbage

   _____3 pounds of celery

   _____6 ½ pounds of unpeeled eggplant

L.O. 16.5

7. Use the same table to determine the amount that must be purchased in order to yield the following EP amounts.

   _____2 pounds of trimmed leeks

   _____8 ounces of sliced mushrooms

   _____9 ounces of chopped onion

   _____1 ½ pounds of sliced green pepper

   _____8 pounds of peeled, sliced potatoes

L.O. 16.5

8. Why is batch cooking important in vegetable cooking?

_____

_____

_____

L.O. 16.7

9. What are three signs that canned foods are damaged and should be discarded?

   • _____

   • _____

   • _____

L.O. 16.6

Chapter 16 Check-in

1. When a vegetable is said to be "al dente," it is
   A. soft.
   B. discolored, due to improper cooking.
   C. firm to the bite.
   D. starchy.

   L.O. 16.3

2. A vegetable is said to be done when
   A. it reaches a certain temperature.
   B. it reaches the desired degree of tenderness.
   C. its fiber has been broken down completely by the cooking process.
   D. it has released all of its nutrients into its cooking liquid.

   L.O. 16.2

3. Chefs often add pieces of apple to red cabbage during cooking because the apples
   A. enhance the color of the cabbage.
   B. reduce the cooking odor of the cabbage.
   C. decrease the cooking time.
   D. reduce the strong flavor of the cabbage.

   L.O. 16.1

4. If the AP weight of Swiss chard is 20 pounds and the yield is 85%, what is the EP weight?
   A. 9 pounds
   B. 17 pounds
   C. 20 pounds
   D. 24 pounds

   L.O. 16.5

5. Three of the following observations may indicate that a shipment of frozen vegetables is of below-standard quality. Which one does not?
   A. Freezer burn
   B. Large ice crystals
   C. Frost
   D. Temperature warmer than 0°F (–18°C)

   L.O. 16.6

CHAPTER 17

COOKING VEGETABLES

Learning Objectives

After reading this chapter, you should be able to:

17.1   Identify vegetables that are well suited to the different vegetable cooking methods.

17.2   Cook vegetables by boiling and steaming.

17.3   Cook vegetables by sautéing and pan-frying.

17.4   Cook vegetables by braising.

17.5   Cook vegetables by baking.

17.6   Cook vegetables by broiling and grilling.

17.7   Cook vegetables by deep-frying.

Chapter 17 Study Outline

1. Boiling and steaming are the most frequently used methods for cooking vegetables.
   - Unless they are to be served immediately, these vegetables are often **shocked** or **refreshed**, drained and then cooled quickly under cold water.
   - Sometimes products cooked by these methods are finished by another, final, method.
2. The main difference between sautéing and pan-frying is the amount of fat used and the cooking times.
3. Stir-frying is similar to sautéing, except that the pan is not moved and the items being cooked are stirred and flipped in hot fat.
4. Braised vegetables tend to be more complex than those that are boiled or steamed, and the cooking times are longer.
5. Baking vegetables usually involves either:
   - Cooking larger starchy vegetables in the oven from the raw to finished state because that produces a desirable texture.
   - Finishing casseroles that are vegetable combinations.

6. Grilling is used to cook certain vegetables quickly, and broiling is used to brown or glaze the tops of vegetables that are cooked or partly cooked.

7. Most vegetables large enough to coat with breading or batter may be deep-fried.

Chapter 17 Exercises

1. What cooking method is used to prepare each of the following?

_____(1) Creamed vegetables

_____(2) Sauerkraut

_____(3) Peas à la Française

_____(4) Glazed sweet potatoes

_____(5) Vegetable and fruit fritters

L.O. 17.1, 17.2, 17.4, 17.5, 17.7

2. What type of vegetable is best suited to broiling?

_____

_____

L.O. 17.6

3. Describe each of the following.
   (1) Shocking

_____

_____

   (2) Ratatouille

_____

_____

L.O. 17.2, 17.4

4. When steaming vegetables in a pressure steamer, what safety precaution must be taken before opening the door?

_____

_____

_____

L.O. 17.2

5. How does stir-frying differ from sautéing?

L.O. 17.3

6. How does pan-frying differ from sautéing?

_____

_____

_____

L.O. 17.3

Chapter 17 Check-in

1. What does the term "shock" mean when applied to vegetable cooking?

   A. To sauté a vegetable before boiling it
   B. To cool a vegetable quickly, such as in cold water, as soon as it is cooked
   C. To start cooking a vegetable by dropping it into rapidly boiling water
   D. To cook a vegetable in a microwave

   L.O. 17.2

2. Which of the following cooking methods does stir-frying most closely resemble?

   A. Sautéing
   B. Pan-frying
   C. Braising
   D. Deep-frying

   L.O. 17.3

3. Which of the following dishes can be described as a braised vegetable dish?

   A. Spinach timbales
   B. Pea fritters
   C. Artichokes clamart
   D. Ratatouille

   L.O. 17.4

4. A croquette is a

   A. vegetable dipped in batter and deep-fried.
   B. mixture of batter and vegetables that is dropped into frying fat by spoonfuls and fried until golden.
   C. thick mixture that is shaped, breaded, and deep-fried.
   D. mixture of vegetables covered with a sauce and browned under a salamander.

   L.O. 17.7

5. Which of the following vegetables is not likely to be cooked by baking?

   A. Asparagus
   B. Winter squash
   C. Potatoes
   D. Sweet potatoes

   L.O. 17.1, 17.5

Chapter 18 Exercises

1. Match each numbered characteristic with the lettered potato variety it describes.

    _____(1) Inappropriate for deep-frying

    _____(2) Large and irregularly shaped

    _____(3) Small and round in shape

    _____(4) Best variety for mashing

    _____(5) Best variety for baking

    _____(6) Contains much moisture, much sugar, and little starch

    _____(7) May be red, white, yellow, or blue

    _____(8) Also called chef's potatoes

    _____(9) Good for mashing but usually too expensive

    _____(10) Best for boiling whole

a. Waxy (new)
b. Russet (Idaho)
c. All-purpose

L.O. 18.1

2. Indicate which of the following are signs of good quality (G) and which are signs of poor quality (P) in potatoes.

    _____Sprouts   _____Green spots

    _____Smooth skin   _____Shallow eyes

    _____Cracks

L.O. 18.2

3. Describe what a tournéed vegetable looks like.

    _____

    _____

    _____

L.O. 18.3

4. What spice characterizes Hungarian potatoes?

    _____

    _____

L.O. 18.3

5. What is done to potatoes when baking to give them crisp skins?

    _____

    _____

    _____

L.O. 18.5

6. What three starches can be used to prepare potato pancakes?

    *   _____

    *   _____

    *   _____

L.O. 18.5

7. Pont-neuf potatoes, allumette potatoes, straw potatoes, and gaufrette potatoes are all variations of what potato recipe?

    _____

L.O. 18.5

8. Match each numbered grain with its lettered description.

_____(1) Enriched rice
_____(2) Short-grain rice
_____(3) Long-grain rice
_____(4) Converted rice
_____(5) Instant rice
_____(6) Brown rice
_____(7) Arborio rice
_____(8) Basmati rice
_____(9) Glutinous rice
_____(10) Wild rice
_____(11) Barley
_____(12) Cracked wheat
_____(13) Bulgur
_____(14) Couscous
_____(15) Hominy
_____(16) Kasha

a. Rice with its bran layer left on it
b. Grain commonly used in soups
c. Very long-grain rice used in Indian cooking
d. Rice with small kernels that become sticky when cooked
e. Partially cooked cracked wheat
f. Rice that has been precooked and dried for quick preparation
g. Rice that has received a coating of nutrients
h. Sweet short-grain rice used in Chinese and Japanese cooking
i. Whole buckwheat groats
j. Long-grain rice that has been partially cooked, dried, and then milled
k. Italian short-grain rice used to make risotto
l. Rice with long, slender grains that become fluffy when cooked
m. Whole wheat that has been cut into smaller pieces
n. Kind of grass grown in the United States
o. Corn that has been treated with lye
p. Wheat product similar to granular pasta

L.O. 18.6

12. The main kinds of salad dressings are oil and vinegar (unthickened), mayonnaise-based (thickened), and cooked (like mayonnaise but tart with little or no oil).

13. Most salad dressings are **emulsions**: uniform mixtures of unmixable liquids.

   - Generally, the harder the mixture is beaten or shaken and the smaller the droplets, the longer the emulsion lasts.

   - Oil and vinegar dressings are temporary emulsions which separate and must be remixed.

   - The egg yolk in mayonnaise dressings coats droplets, keeping them in suspension, which makes the emulsion permanent.

Chapter 19 Exercises

1. Suggest three accompaniment salads for each of the following main courses. Explain your choices.

   a. Baked chicken with rice pilaf and steamed carrots

      - _____

      - _____

      - _____

   b. Home-style meat loaf with boiled potatoes and green beans

      - _____

      - _____

      - _____

L.O. 19.1

2. Match each numbered characteristic with the lettered salad green it describes.

_____(1) Essential for Caesar salad

_____(2) Often served as a vegetable in Italian cuisine

_____(3) Has a delicate, nutty flavor

_____(4) Mixture of tender, baby lettuces

_____(5) Most popular salad ingredient

_____(6) Best in spring

_____(7) Spearhead-shaped green; often served alone

_____(8) Red-leafed, Italian variety of chicory

_____(9) Cup-shaped leaves ideal for salad bases

_____(10) Most commonly used as a garnish

a. Boston lettuce
b. Mesclun
c. Iceberg lettuce
d. Watercress
e. Dandelion greens
f. Belgian endive
g. Mâche
h. Radicchio
i. Escarole or broad-leaf endive
j. Romaine lettuce

L.O. 19.2

3. The Corner Grill serves a signature salad composed of marinated kidney beans, artichoke hearts, and onions over romaine lettuce, topped with tarragon vinaigrette and black olives.

(1) Which ingredient(s) makes up the base?

_____

(2) Which ingredient(s) makes up the body?

_____

(3) Which ingredient(s) makes up the garnish?

_____

(4) Which ingredient(s) makes up the dressing?

_____

L.O. 19.4

4. Match each numbered salad with its lettered primary ingredients.

_____(1) Caesar salad

_____(2) Coleslaw

_____(3) Waldorf salad

_____(4) Chef's salad

_____(5) Salade Niçoise

a. Mixed greens, turkey strips, ham strips, cheese strips, tomatoes, hard-cooked eggs

b. Romaine lettuce, bread cubes, anchovies, eggs, and parmesan cheese

c. Potatoes, green beans, greens, tuna, anchovies, olives, hard-cooked eggs

d. Cabbage, mayonnaise

e. Apples, celery, walnuts, chantilly dressing

L.O. 19.7

5. Invent a salad using five different ingredients. Describe what type of salad it is (appetizer, accompaniment, etc.) and name the components of its base, body, garnish, and dressing.

_____

_____

_____

_____

L.O. 19.4, 19,7

6. Indicate whether each dressing below is an oil and vinegar dressing (O/V) or a mayonnaise-based dressing (M).

_____(1) Thousand Island

_____(2) Basic French

_____(3) Chantilly

_____(4) Blue cheese

_____(5) Italian

L.O. 19.10

7. Name five examples of different vinegar that can be used to prepare salad dressings.

- _____
- _____
- _____
- _____
- _____

L.O. 19.9

Chapter 19 Check-in

1. Which of the following has the crispest texture?

   A. Boston lettuce
   B. Loose-leaf lettuce
   C. Iceberg lettuce
   D. Bibb lettuce

   L.O. 19.2

2. For serving as a main course at lunch, which of the following types of salads likely would be the most appropriate?

   A. Combination salad
   B. Green salad
   C. Gelatin salad
   D. Vegetable salad

   L.O. 19.1

3. Potatoes, green beans, tuna, olives, and hard-cooked eggs are some of the main ingredients in

   A. salade niçoise.
   B. oriental salad.
   C. chef's salad.
   D. Waldorf salad.

   L.O. 19.7

4. Winterized oil is

   A. oil that must be kept refrigerated.
   B. oil that has been treated so that it remains clear and liquid at low temperatures.
   C. another name for extra virgin olive oil.
   D. corn oil made from corn grown in a cold climate.

   L.O. 19.9

5. Which of the following is a permanent emulsion?

   A. Vinaigrette
   B. Italian dressing
   C. Honey lemon dressing
   D. Mayonnaise

   L.O. 19.10

CHAPTER 20

SANDWICHES AND HORS D'OEUVRES

Learning Objectives

After reading this chapter, you should be able to:

20.1   Describe the desirable qualities in sandwich bread; provide examples of specific types of bread well suited for preparing sandwiches; and list six measures that can be taken to ensure freshness in bread.

20.2   State three purposes of sandwich spreads; and identify guidelines for the use of butter and mayonnaise as spreads.

20.3   Identify the most popular types of sandwich fillings.

20.4   Set up an efficient sandwich station.

20.5   List a dozen popular cold sandwich combinations.

20.6   Prepare simple, cold sandwiches in quantity.

20.7   Prepare canapés and other popular categories of hors d'oeuvres.

Chapter 20 Study Outline

1. Among the many kinds of breads used in the pantry department to make sandwiches, pullman (sandwich) loaves are used most frequently.

2. Butter, mayonnaise, and other spreads are used to add flavor and moisture to sandwiches and to keep the filling from making the bread soggy.

3. Sandwich fillings include meats, poultry, cheese, fish and shellfish, mayonnaise-based salads, and vegetables.

4. There is a variety of sandwich types.
    - Hot sandwiches can be simple, open-faced, grilled, or deep-fried.
    - Cold sandwiches include multidecker, open-faced, and tea varieties.

5. Ingredients and equipment at the sandwich station should be set up for efficiency, sanitation, and portion control.

6. Most sandwiches are cut before serving for easy handling and attractive presentation.

7. Hors d'oeuvres are small, spicy finger foods eaten—often with drinks—apart from the main meal as appetizers or served at receptions.

8. **Canapés** are bite-size open-faced sandwich hors d'oeuvres constructed with a base, such as bread or crackers, a spread, and a garnish.

9. Non-drink appetizer cocktails include fruit preparations and chilled seafood, usually served with a tangy sauce.

10. Various raw vegetables and pickled items—relishes—are often served as appetizers.

11. Proper consistency is important in dip preparation.

Chapter 20 Exercises

1. How should sandwich bread (other than hard-crusted varieties) be stored?

    _____

    _____

    _____

L.O. 20.1

2. Match each dip or hors d'oeuvre on the left with its primary ingredients on the right.

    _____(1) Hummus

    _____(2) Guacamole

    _____(3) Crêpes

    _____(4) Boreks

    _____(5) Chicken satay

    a. Avocado, onion, chili pepper, lime or lemon juice
    b. Chickpeas, tahini, garlic, lemon juice, olive oil
    c. Garlic, ginger root, soy sauce, chicken breast, peanut butter
    d. Flour, salt, eggs, milk, browned butter
    e. Feta cheese, phyllo dough

L.O. 20.7

3. What are the meat ingredients in the following sandwiches?

   (1) Monte cristo

_____

_____

   (2) Reuben

_____

_____

   (3) Club

_____

_____

L.O. 20.3, 20.5

4. What are the two most commonly used spreads for sandwiches?

   • _____

   • _____

L.O. 20.2

5. List four different items that can be used as bases for canapés.

   • _____

   • _____

   • _____

   • _____

L.O. 20.7

Chapter 20 Check-in

1. Which of the following is the least
   desirable way to store bread?

   A. Keeping it in the refrigerator
   B. Keeping it in the freezer
   C. Keeping it tightly wrapped
   D. Keeping it at room temperature

   L.O. 20.1

2. Which of the following is not one of
   the main purposes of a spread in a
   sandwich?

   A. To add flavor
   B. To protect the bread from the
      moisture of the filling
   C. To provide moisture or "mouth
      feel"
   D. To help the filling stick to the
      bread

   L.O. 20.2

3. Which of the following is not usually
   a sandwich filling?

   A. vegetable items
   B. shellfish
   C. mayonnaise-based salads
   D. gelatin-based salads

   L.O. 20.3

4. A raw vegetable item served as an
   hors d'oeuvre is called a

   A. cocktail.
   B. crudité.
   C. dipper.
   D. canapé.

   L.O. 20.7

5. Which of the following is not
   normally an ingredient in a reuben
   sandwich?

   A. Sauerkraut
   B. Russian dressing
   C. Sliced turkey
   D. Sliced corned beef

   L.O. 20.5

CHAPTER 21

BREAKFAST PREPARATION, DAIRY PRODUCTS, AND COFFEE AND TEA

Learning Objectives

After reading this chapter, you should be able to:

21.1   Describe the composition of eggs and the major differences among grades.

21.2   Store eggs.

21.3   Prepare the following egg items and egg-based dishes: hard-, medium-, and soft-cooked eggs; poached eggs; fried eggs; shirred eggs, scrambled eggs; omelets; entrée soufflés; and savory custards.

21.4   List the key differences between waffle batter and pancake batter, and prepare each.

21.5   Prepare French toast, and identify the common variations possible by changing the basic ingredients.

21.6   Prepare each of the two general types of cooked cereals.

21.7   Identify the three most common breakfast meats and prepare them.

21.8   Describe the major milk, cream, and butter products.

21.9   Explain why milk curdles and why it scorches, and identify the steps to take to keep each from occurring.

21.10   Identify the guidelines for achieving the best results when whipping cream.

21.11   Identify eight general varieties of cheeses most commonly used in the commercial kitchen, and provide an example of each.

21.12   Identify general storage and serving guidelines for cheeses.

21.13   Identify five guidelines for cooking with cheese.

21.14   Describe nine basic principles of making coffee.

21.15   Explain the correct procedures for making hot tea and iced tea.

Chapter 21 Study Outline

1. High heat and long cooking toughen eggs and adversely affect their color and flavor.
2. Methods for cooking eggs include:
   - Simmering in the shell
   - Poaching
   - Frying
   - Shirring
   - Scrambled
   - Omelets: French, American style, fluffy, flat
   - Soufflés
   - Stirred and baked custards and quiches
3. Pancakes and waffles are cooked to order and served hot.
4. French toast is made from slices of bread dipped in a batter of eggs, milk, sugar, and flavorings.
5. The two types of cooked cereals are (1) whole, cracked, or flaked and (2) granular.
6. Cold, dry cereals are bought ready-prepared.
7. The meats that appear on most breakfast menus are bacon, ham, and sausage.
8. Milk and cream fall into various categories.
   - Fresh milk can be whole, pasteurized, raw, certified, or homogenized and includes skim, low-fat, fortified, and flavored.
   - Cream might be of the following forms: whipping, light, or crème fraîche.
   - Fermented milk products include sour cream, buttermilk, and yogurt.
   - Milk products with water removed include evaporated, condensed, or dried milk.
9. Problems in cooking milk and cream products include curdling, scorching, and skin formation.
10. Butter consists of 80% milk fat.
    - Butter is the preferred cooking fat for most purposes, especially sauce making.
    - Butter should be kept well wrapped since it absorbs odors and flavors easily.
11. The preliminary form of cheese is milk solids separated from the liquid by the curdling action of rennet enzyme added to milk.
12. Certain bacteria or molds introduced during manufacturing ripen cheese and change its flavor and texture.
    - Cheeses are classified according to the kind of ripener used and whether it ripens from the outside or inside.
    - They are also classified by the amount of fat they contain.

13. For many people, the quality of the coffee is the most important factor in choosing where to dine.
    - Many standard and special-purpose varieties and blends are available in a range of qualities and prices.
    - The flavor of coffee deteriorates quickly after about an hour of holding.
14. Variations in processing tea produce three categories.
    - Black tea is fermented by allowing freshly harvested leaves to oxidize in a damp place.
    - Green tea is dried without fermenting.
    - Oolong tea is partially fermented to a greenish-brown color.

Chapter 21 Exercises

1. Number the following egg sizes from smallest (1) to largest (6).

_____Medium   _____Small

_____Jumbo   _____Large

_____Peewee

_____Extra Large

L.O. 21.1

2. What cooking method is used to prepare soft-cooked, medium-cooked, and hard-cooked eggs?

   (1) Soft cooked

   _____

   _____

   (2) Medium cooked

   _____

   _____

   (3) Hard cooked

   _____

   _____

L.O. 21.3

3. Match each numbered egg recipe description with the lettered cooking method used below.

_____(1) Beaten eggs cooked in a buttered sauté pan and stirred as they cook

_____(2) Whole eggs cooked in gently bubbling water

_____(3) Shelled eggs baked in individual serving dishes

_____(4) Beaten egg whites baked with a béchamel sauce and cheese, vegetables, seafood, or other ingredients

_____(4) Unshelled, unbeaten eggs cooked in gently bubbling water

_____(5) Beaten eggs mixed with a liquid and cooked until coagulated

_____(6) Beaten eggs cooked without stirring in a special pan and folded over

_____(7) Whole shelled eggs cooked on a buttered griddle

a. Simmered in the shell
b. Poached
c. Fried
d. Shirred
e. Scrambled
f. Omelet
g. Soufflé
h. Custard

L.O. 21.3

4. What will minimize shrinkage of bacon?

_____

_____

_____

L.O. 21.7

5. Match each milk product on the left with its description on the right.

_____(1) Whole milk
_____(2) Pasteurized milk
_____(3) Raw milk
_____(4) Homogenized milk
_____(5) Skim milk
_____(6) Fortified milk
_____(7) Whipping cream
_____(8) Sour cream
_____(9) Buttermilk
_____(10) Yogurt
_____(11) Evaporated milk
_____(12) Condensed milk
_____(13) Dried milk

a. Cultured cream that is thick and tastes tangy
b. Milk with 60% of its water removed and sweetened with sugar
c. Milk cultured with a special strain of bacteria
d. Milk processed so that the cream will not separate
e. Milk, with nothing removed and only vitamin D added
f. Milk with most of its fat removed
g. Milk in powder form
h. Cream with 30 to 40% fat
i. Milk that has been heated to kill disease-causing bacteria
j. Milk used in recipes calling for "sour milk"
k. Unsweetened milk with 60% of its water removed
l. Milk with added nutrients
m. Milk that has not been pasteurized (illegal in most cases)

L.O. 21.8

6. Match each cheese on the left with its category on the right. Each letter will be used twice.

_____(1) Cream
_____(2) Blue
_____(3) Limburger
_____(4) Camembert
_____(5) Liederkranz
_____(6) Gouda
_____(7) Brie
_____(8) Cottage
_____(9) Roquefort
_____(10) Swiss

a. Ripened from the inside with bacteria
b. Ripened from the outside with bacteria
c. Ripened from the inside with mold
d. Ripened from the outside with mold
e. Unripened

L.O. 21.11

7. Match each cheese on the left with its native country on the right.

     _____(1) Edam   a.   France
     _____(2) Stilton   b.   Italy
     _____(3) Saga Bleu   c.   England
     _____(4) Romano   d.   Greece
     _____(5) Appenzeller   e.   The Netherlands
     _____(6) Feta   f.   Switzerland
     _____(7) Port Salut   g.   Denmark

L.O. 21.11

8. What is the primary difference between a process cheese and a cold pack cheese?

_____

_____

_____

L.O. 21.11

9. Which type of batter is usually thicker in texture, waffle batter or pancake batter? Why?

_____

_____

_____

L.O. 21.4

10. What is the simplest way to avoid scorching milk when heating it on the stovetop?

_____

_____

_____

L.O. 21.9

11. Before whipping heavy cream, you should make sure that the cream and the equipment are at what temperature for best results?

_____

L.O. 21.10

12. Cheese has its best flavor and texture at what serving temperature?

_____

L.O. 21.12

Chapter 21 Check-in

1. The three USDA egg grades are
    A. A, B, and C.
    B. A, B, and Utility.
    C. AA, A, and B.
    D. A Plus, A, and A Minus.
   L.O. 21.1

2. At approximately what temperature does a custard mixture (whole eggs and milk) coagulate?
    A. 145°F (63°C)
    B. 165°F (74°C)
    C. 185°F (85°C)
    D. 212°F (100°C)
   L.O. 21.3

3 What is the fat content of heavy cream?
    A. 10–12%
    B. 16–22%
    C. 28–33%
    D. 35–40%
   L.O. 21.8

4. Which of the following is not one of the major causes of curdling in milk?
    A. Acids
    B. Freezing
    C. Tannins
    D. Heat
   L.O. 21.9

5. To make coffee of normal strength, how much water is used per pound of coffee?
    A. 2 quarts (2 liters)
    B. 1 gallon (4 liters)
    C. 2 gallons (8 liters)
    D. 3 gallons (12 liters)
   L.O. 21.14

CHAPTER 22

Learning Objectives

After reading this chapter, you should be able to:

22.1   Prepare simple dry-cured and brine cured foods.

22.2   Describe three steps involved in preparing simple smoked foods.

22.3   Explain the differences among fresh, cured, and smoked sausages, and describe the basic procedures for their preparation.

Chapter 22 Study Outline

1. Curing and smoking are traditional techniques used to **preserve** foods and to **change their flavor**.

2. The most important ingredients used in curing are salt, nitrites and nitrates, sugar, and flavoring ingredients such as herbs and spices.

    *   Curing with **salt** decreases the moisture content of foods and increase their salt content. This makes the food less hospitable to bacteria growth.

    *   **Nitrites and nitrates** help guard meats against botulism. Meats cured with these chemicals remain red when cooked.

    *   **Sugars** are sometimes included in cure mixtures to help increase the moistness of cured foods.

    *   Different **spice mixtures** give characteristic flavors to different cured foods.

3. The two basic types of cures are **dry cures** and **brines.**

4. Meats, poultry, and fish should be cured before being smoked, in order to guard against food-borne disease.

5. The two basic types of smoking are **cold smoking** and **hot smoking**.
   - In cold smoking, the temperature inside the smokehouse is kept at or below 85°F (30°C). Cold-smoked foods are still raw after smoking.
   - In hot smoking, the temperature inside the smokehouse may be as high as 165°F(74°C) for sausage and meats, or as high as 200°F (93°C). Foods may be hot-smoked until cooked, or they may be partially cooked in the smoker and then simmered until fully cooked.

6. A typical smoker consists of the following elements:
   - Enclosed chamber for holding the foods to be smoked
   - Source of smoke
   - Means to circulate the smoke around the food
   - Way to control the temperature in the smoking chamber

7. Sausages can be classified as **fresh, cured,** and **smoked.** Smoked sausages are also cured.

8. The basic ingredients of sausage meat are the following:
   - Lean pork
   - Pork fat
   - Salt
   - Spices, herbs, and other seasonings and flavorings

9. For cured and smoked sausages, the curing salt (nitrites and/or nitrates) are mixed with the ground meat.

10. Natural casings are made from the intestines of sheep, hogs, and beef. Collagen casings are artificial casings made from animal products and therefore edible. Synthetic casings are not edible.

11. The type of grind determines the texture of the sausage.

Chapter 22 Exercises

1. Match each numbered item with the lettered description that best fits it.

    _____(1)   Charcuterie
    _____(2)   Curing salt
    _____(3)   Natural casing
    _____(4)   Nitrosamine
    _____(5)   Brine
    _____(6)   Cold smoking
    _____(7)   Sodium nitrite
    _____(8)   Smoked sausage
    _____(9)   Certified pork
    _____(10) Quatre épices

a. Less than 85°F (30°C)
b. Curing agent in Prague Powder #1
c. Made from animal intestines
d. Cured before smoked
e. Art of preparing products such as sausages, pâtés, and smoked ham
f. Strong salt water solution
g. Tinted curing mix
h. Spice mixture in some sausages
i. Formed when meat containing nitrate is cooked at high heat
j. Free of trichinosis

L.O. 22.1–22.3

2. Why is it important to cure meats before smoking them?

_____

_____

_____

L.O. 22.2

3. What is the difference in texture between a regular grind sausage and an emulsified grind sausage?

_____

_____

_____

L.O. 22.3

4. What is the main factor that determines how long a meat must rest in a brine cure?

_____

L.O. 22.1

5. Describe how to prepare natural sausage casings for stuffing, up until threading them on the sausage stuffing nozzle.

_____

_____

_____

L.O. 22.3

Chapter 22 Check-in

1. Curing salt, or Prague Powder #1, consists of table salt and

   A. sodium nitrate.
   B. sodium nitrite.
   C. potassium nitrate.
   D. potassium nitrite.

   L.O. 22.1

2. Nitrates are used mainly in

   A. bacon.
   B. fresh sausages.
   C. air-dried sausages and hams.
   D. None of the above are correct.

   L.O. 22.1

3. What is the most important reason to cure meats before smoking them?

   A. Improve the flavor
   B. Prevent foods from being overcooked by the heat of the smoke
   C. Guard against foodborne disease
   D. None of the above are correct.

   L.O. 22.2

4. Which of the following statements about fresh sausages is incorrect?

   A. Fresh sausages contain no nitrites.
   B. Simple fresh sausage meat consists of ground meat and fat plus seasonings and flavorings.
   C. Fresh sausages, by definition, are never hot-smoked.
   D. None of the above. Meats are not cured before being smoked.

   L.O. 22.3

5. What is the preferred fat to use in most sausages?

   A. Rendered lard
   B. Hard fatback
   C. Beef suet
   D. Unsmoked bacon

   L.O. 22.3

CHAPTER 23

PÂTÉS, TERRINES, AND OTHER COLD FOODS

Learning Objectives

After reading this chapter, you should be able to:

23.1   Prepare classic aspic jelly and regular aspic jelly, and explain how to use them to create finished dishes.

23.2   Prepare classic chaud-froid and mayonnaise chaud-froid, and use them to create finished dishes.

23.3   Prepare poultry livers for use in forcemeats.

23.4   Prepare basic meat and poultry forcemeats.

23.5   Explain the similarities and differences between terrines and pâtés.

23.6   Prepare terrines and pâtés using basic forcemeats.

23.7   Prepare a chicken galantine.

23.8   Prepare basic mousseline forcemeats.

23.9   Make terrines using basic mousseline forcemeats.

23.10 Prepare specialty terrines and other molded dishes based on aspics and mousses.

23.11 Handle raw foie gras and explain how to prepare a terrine of foie gras.

23.12 Prepare baked liver terrines.

23.13 Prepare a typical rillettes.

Chapter 23 Study Outline

1. Good food handling practices and careful sanitation are important in the preparation of cold foods because they might be handled extensively and not cooked again to kill organisms before being served.

2. Appearance is a primary consideration in the production of cold foods. Follow guidelines for attractive food presentation.

3. **Aspic jelly** is a clarified stock that contains enough gelatin so that it solidifies when cold. It is used to coat many kinds of cold foods to protect them from air and to enhance their appearance. It is also used as ingredient in some terrine molds.

   - The gelatin in aspic may be extracted as part of stock making, or it may be added in the form of packaged gelatin.
   - Stock for aspic must be clarified for best appearance.

4. **Chaud-froid** is a thick white sauce containing gelatin. It is used to coat some cold foods.

   - Classical chaud-froid is an aspic jelly with the addition of cream or a liaison.
   - Mayonnaise chaud-froid is mayonnaise combined with aspic jelly.

5. A **forcemeat** is a mixture of seasoned, ground meats used as a stuffing or filling.

   - A straight forcemeat is a mixture of seasoned, ground meat and fat in varying proportions.
   - A country-style forcemeat is a straight forcemeat with a coarse grind. It usually contains some liver.
   - A gratin forcemeat contains some partially cooked meat. It usually contains an additional binding agent calade a **panada.**
   - A mousseline forcemeat consists of a white meat or seafood processed to a fine purée and combined with heavy cream and egg.

6. Livers used in forcemeats are liquefied and strained.

7. A terrine is a forcemeat baked in a mold, such as an earthenware dish.

8. A pâté is a forcemeat baked in a crust.

9. A galantine is a forcemeat that is wrapped in the skin of the product it is made from, such as a chicken or duck.

10. Specialty terrines include baked terrines made with a mousseline forcemeat plus garnish, and unbaked terrines made with gelatine-based ingredients such as aspics and mousses.

11. Foie gras is the fatted liver of specially fed varieties of ducks and geese. It is high in price and demands careful preparation and handling.

12. Basic liver terrines, such as chicken liver terrines, consist of liquidized, strained livers, plus eggs, starch, cream or another source of fat, and seasonings. They are baked until the liquid mixture has set.

13. Classic rillettes is a dish made of pork cooked with seasonings until very tender, shredded, mixed with its own fat, and chilled. It is served as a savory spread. Similar products may be made with other meats and even seafood.

Chapter 23 Exercises

1. Match each numbered item with the lettered description that best fits it.

    _____(1) Mousse
    _____(2) Aspic jelly
    _____(3) Chaud-froid
    _____(4) Pâté de campagne
    _____(5) Galantine
    _____(6) Garde manger
    _____(7) Forcemeat
    _____(8) Terrine
    _____(9) Grillettes

a. Ground meat used as a filling
b. Country-style
c. Name means "hot and cold"
d. Forcemeat rolled in a skin
e. Clarified stock set with gelatin
f. Pantry
g. Fatty meat spread
h. Lightened with whipped cream and set with gelatin
i. Paté without a crust

L.O. 23.1–23.2, 23.4–23.9, 23.11

2. If you want to make a stock that you can use for aspic jelly, what kinds of ingredients should you include so that you will not need to add packaged gelatin to strengthen the aspic? Give some examples.

_____

_____

_____

_____

_____

L.O. 23.1

3. What is the difference between a straight forcemeat and a country-style forcemeat?

_____

_____

_____

L.O. 23.4

4. What is the preferred fat to use in a straight forcemeat?

_____

_____

L.O. 23.4

5. List the five steps in preparing poultry livers for forcemeats.

- _____

- _____

- _____

- _____

- _____

L.O. 23.3

6. List three reasons for covering a baked terrine with a layer of aspic after it has cooled.

- _____

- _____

- _____

L.O. 23.5

7. The amount of cream used in a mousseline varies depending on how you are going to use the mousseline. For which product can you use more cream, a terrine that is to be sliced or a small mold to be served whole as a single portion? Why?

_____

_____

_____

L.O. 23.7

8. What are the four basic steps in preparing a terrine from a savory cold mousse?

    • _____

    • _____

    • _____

    • _____

L.O. 23.8

9. Why is flour added to the mixture for making a chicken liver terrine?

    _____

    _____

    _____

    _____

L.O. 23.10

Chapter 23 Check-in

1. If you have made a veal stock that sets firm when it is chilled, what must you do to it to make it into an aspic jelly?

   A. Degrease it.
   B. Clarify and degrease it.
   C. Clarify and degrease it and fortify it with powdered gelatin.
   D. None of the above are correct.

   L.O. 23.1

2. Mayonnaise chaud-froid consists of

   A. mayonnaise and aspic jelly.
   B. mayonnaise, white stock, gelatin, and a liaison.
   C. mayonnaise, velouté, and aspic jelly.
   D. mayonnaise, aspic jelly, and heavy cream.

   L.O. 23.2

3. Which of the following is not one of the steps in the basic procedure for preparing poultry livers for forcemeats?

   A. Soak in milk for 24 hours.
   B. Drain and salt the livers and refrigerate for several hours.
   C. Liquefy in a blender.
   D. Strain to remove connective tissue.

   L.O. 23.3

4. A straight pork forcemeat that is made with a coarse grind and some liver is a

   A. gratin forcemeat.
   B. panada.
   C. mousseline forcemeat.
   D. country-style forcemeat.

   L.O. 23.4

5. The basic difference between a terrine and a pâté is that a pâté is

   A. baked in a crust, and a terrine is not.
   B. smooth and spreadable, and a terrine is firm and sliceable.
   C. made with liver, and a terrine is not.
   D. None of the above are correct.

   L.O. 23.5

CHAPTER 24

FOOD PRESENTATION AND GARNISH

Learning Objectives

After reading this chapter, you should be able to:

24.1   Explain why attractive food presentation is important.

24.2   Serve food that is attractively arranged on the plate or platter, with proper balance of color, shape, and texture.

24.3   Identify common terms from classical garniture that are still in general use today.

24.4   Garnish a banquet platter with attractive and appropriate vegetable accompaniments.

24.5   Prepare simple garnishes out of common fruits and vegetables using decorative techniques.

24.6   Plan and arrange attractive food platters for buffets.

Chapter 24 Study Outline

1. Appearance is important to the service of food because it affects diners' feelings of satisfaction with the meal. Interesting, successful food presentation depends on proper cooking, carefulness and neatness, and knowledge of presentation principles and techniques.

2. Food should be arranged on the plate simply but with care as a picture with the plate rim as the frame.

    - The selection of foods and garnishes should have balance and harmony of colors, shapes, textures, and flavors.

    - Portion sizes of the items should be balanced—though not necessarily the same—and should be matched to the plate to avoid appearing skimpy or overcrowded.

    - The most common pattern is placing the meat or fish item closest to the diner and the vegetable and starch items at the rear, but cooks and chefs can create many others.

    - Serve hot foods hot on hot plates, and serve cold foods cold on cold plates.

3. Garnishes need not be elaborate or difficult to prepare.
   - Sometimes accompaniments provide enough color and balance, and no garnish is needed.
   - A simple garnish should be appropriate to the food, edible, and planned; you should not use the same garnish on every plate.
4. A variety of techniques can add decorative touches to food presentation.
5. Buffet service is popular with customers, and it is efficient and adaptable for foodservice operations.
   - The appearance of a buffet sells the food.
   - Color, height, spacing, orderliness, and other factors go into creating a buffet that has a look of abundance but is still simple.
6. The cocktail buffet serves only appetizer-type foods.
   - Stacks of small plates are placed beside each item.
   - The table(s) should be centrally located in the room.
7. Designing a platter involves a focal point, movement, proportion, and placement of food items.
   - It is useful to sketch a design as you plan.
   - Cheese platters are designed differently, using large pieces or whole cheeses and sometimes fresh fruit.
   - Keep food sanitation in mind when planning and handling cold buffet presentations.
8. Hot foods for buffets are usually served from chafing dishes and must rely on their nicely-cooked appearance and smell to attract customers rather than on decoration or garnish.
   - The foods should be easily portioned or already portioned.
   - They are best placed at the end of the buffet, after cold platters.

Chapter 24 Exercises

1. Describe the arrangement of a plate, including a vegetable, starch, and/or garnish, around each of the following entrées.

    (1) Sole vin blanc

    _____

    _____

    _____

    (2) Roast rib of beef au jus

    _____

    _____

    _____

    (3) Broiled lamb chop

    _____

    _____

    _____

    (4) Poached chicken breast princesse

    _____

    _____

    _____

    (5) Vegetable lasagna

    _____

    _____

    _____

L.O. 24.2

2. Match each garnish term on the left with its description on the right.

_____(1) Bouquetière
_____(2) Clamart
_____(3) Crécy, Vichy
_____(4) Doria
_____(5) Dubarry
_____(6) Fermière
_____(7) Florentine
_____(8) Forestière
_____(9) Jardinière
_____(10) Judic
_____(11) Lyonnaise
_____(12) Niçoise
_____(13) Parmentier
_____(14) Princesse
_____(15) Printanière
_____(16) Primeurs
_____(17) Provençale

a. Sliced carrots, turnips, onions, and celery
b. Spring vegetables
c. Onions
d. Cucumbers cooked in butter
e. Carrots
f. Garden vegetables
g. Bouquet of vegetables
h. Asparagus
i. Mushrooms
j. Tomatoes, garlic, parsley (sometimes mushrooms, olives)
k. Tomato concassée with garlic
l. Peas
m. Braised lettuce
n. First spring vegetables
o. Cauliflower
p. Potatoes
q. Spinach

L.O. 24.3

3. Plan a buffet service that includes the following items:

Prepared salad   Cheeses
Prepared sandwiches   Breads and crackers
Hot soup   Individual prepared fruit plates

   a. Describe each course.

_____

_____

_____

_____

_____

   b. Describe the arrangement of the serving table, including plates and any centerpiece.

_____

_____

_____

_____

   c. Describe garnishes you will use.

_____

_____

_____

L.O. 24.6

4. Why is the buffet a popular form of food presentation?

_____

_____

_____

L.O. 24.6

5. a. Using the information from text pages 630–635, choose a variety of five to ten cheeses for a cheese platter.

   _____

   _____

   _____

   b. Create a sketch for the design of your cheese platter.

L.O. 24.6

Chapter 24 Check-in

1. An item listed on a menu as Veal Chop Forestière will be garnished with

    A. mushrooms.
    B. rissole potatoes.
    C. caramelized onions.
    D. spinach.

    L.O. 24.3

2. If serving fried chicken with mashed potatoes and gravy, which of the following vegetables would you serve for the best balance on the plate?

    A. Cauliflower
    B. Pearl onions lightly browned in butter
    C. Peas
    D. Glazed turnips

    L.O. 24.2

3. A carefully shaped, oval spoonful of a food item used as a garnish is called a

    A. ravier.
    B. quenelle.
    C. garni.
    D. bouquetière.

    L.O. 24.5

4. Which of the following is not part of a standard buffet platter?

    A. Grosse pièce
    B. Garnish
    C. Main item
    D. Appetizer

    L.O. 24.6

5. Which of the following is least likely to be served as part of a buffet that features cold and hot foods?

    A. Chocolate cake
    B. Chicken stew
    C. Lamb chops
    D. Molded ham mousse

    L.O. 24.6

CHAPTER 25

RECIPES FROM INTERNATIONAL CUISINES

Learning Objectives

After reading this chapter, you should be able to:

25.1   Describe typical ingredients and techniques commonly used in cuisine from Japan, China, Italy, and other European countries.

25.2   Prepare typical international recipes, including: nigirizushi, enchiladas, cipolline in agrodolce, Welsh rabbit, avgolemono, and sauerbraten.

Chapter 25 Study Outline

1. The classical cuisine that descended from the French has been and continues to be influenced by the styles and techniques of other countries and ethnic groups. A dish influenced by another cuisine will not necessarily be identical to a dish genuinely of that cuisine.

2. Japanese cuisine frequently uses simmering, steaming, and grilling for its delicately seasoned foods.

    * Much care is given to appearance—the creation of uncluttered, elegant presentations.
    * The most important food in the Japanese diet is plain rice.
    * Fish dishes are prominent.

3. Chinese cooking is not one style, but a number of regional styles that share some characteristics.

    * The main dish of a meal is usually rice, and other dishes are considered accompaniments for it.
    * Meat is not prominent.
    * For most dishes, cooking time is very short, and preparation time is long.
    * Stir-frying is just one Chinese technique; many other methods are used.

4. The Mexican dishes most familiar in the United States are based on the cuisine of northern Mexico, but cookery of other regions is different and quite varied. Tex-Mex cuisine is based on influences of northern Mexico and the southwestern U.S., which have some cultural history in common.

5. The U.S. cooking style known as Italian represents only part of the cuisine of one region, southern Italy, not the varied styles of all of the country's regions.

    • The cooking of southern Italy is based on olive oil and tomatoes; that of the north is based on butter and cream.

    • Many cooking methods are used in preparing Italian foods, including simmering, grilling, boiling, and frying.

6. Many dishes strongly identified with a number of other European countries have been incorporated into the U.S. cuisine and have become a familiar part of it.

Chapter 25 Exercises

1. What is dashi?

    _____

    _____

    _____

L.O. 25.1

2. Match each food on the left with its country of origin on the right.

    _____(1) Chiles rellenos   a. Spain

    _____(2) Tea-smoked duck   b. Mexico

    _____(3) Moussaka   c. Greece

    _____(4) Polenta   d. Japan

    _____(5) Kappa-maki   e. Italy

    _____(6) Paella   f. China

L.O. 25.2

3. Match each food on the left with its primary ingredients on the right.

_____(1) Polenta

_____(2) Alsa cruda

_____(3) Moussaka

_____(4) Pearl balls

_____(5) Frijoles

_____(6) Chicken teriyaki

_____(7) Chiles rellenos

a. Tomatoes, green chiles, onion, coriander leaves (cilantro), lime juice

b. Beans, onion, garlic, green chile, pork fat

c. Chiles Poblanos, picadillo, batter

d. Cornmeal

e. Glutinous rice, ground pork, scallions, water chestnuts, ginger, soy sauce

f. Ground lamb, eggplant, garlic, tomato

g. Soy sauce, saké, chicken

L.O. 25.1, 25.2

Chapter 25 Check-in

1. What is the most important item in a typical Chinese meal?

   A. Meat
   B. Vegetables
   C. Rice
   D. Seafood

   L.O. 25.1

2. Rice used to make sushi is a

   A. special type of short-grain rice.
   B. special type of long-grain rice.
   C. parboiled rice.
   D. glutinous rice or sticky rice.

   L.O. 25.1

3. Chinese pearl balls are cooked by

   A. stir-frying.
   B. boiling.
   C. stewing.
   D. steaming.

   L.O. 25.2

4. The main ingredients in saltimbocca alla Romana are

   A. veal scaloppine, prosciutto, and sage.
   B. veal chops and fontina cheese.
   C. pork loin, mozzarella cheese, and tomato sauce.
   D. mozzarella cheese, bread, and egg.

   L.O. 25.1, 25.2

5. Cipolline in agrodolce are

   A. sliced onions browned and cooked in wine.
   B. small whole onions cooked with sugar and vinegar.
   C. small whole onions in a light tomato sauce.
   D. roasted peppers in olive oil.

   L.O. 25.2

CHAPTER 26

BAKESHOP PRODUCTION: BASIC PRINCIPLES AND INGREDIENTS

Learning Objectives

After reading this chapter, you should be able to:

26.1   Explain why it is important to weigh baking ingredients.

26.2   Use a baker's balance scale.

26.3   Calculate formulas based on baker's percentages.

26.4   Explain four factors that control the development of gluten in baked products.

26.5   Explain seven changes that take place in a dough or batter as it bakes.

26.6   Utilize three techniques that can prevent or retard the staling of baked items.

26.7   Describe the functions and characteristics of the seven major categories of ingredients in baked goods.

Chapter 26 Study Outline

1. Most bakery products are based on the same few ingredients.
    - Accuracy in measurement and procedures is important in baking because small differences in either can cause large differences in the product.
    - All ingredients must be weighed (scaled).
        - Eggs, milk, and water weigh one pound per pint (or one liter per kilogram), so they may be measured by volume if that is more convenient.
        - Liquid-flavoring ingredients used in very small quantities may also be measured by volume.
2. Bakeshop recipes—called formulas—list ingredients as percentages of the amount of flour to be used.
    - The flour is always 100%, and any ingredient that weighs the same as the flour is also listed as 100%.
    - Formulas are used to convert to higher and lower yields.
    - Baker's formulas are balanced for the specific ingredients listed, so if you substitute others, such as a different kind of flour, the formula might not work well.

3. The structure and strength of baked items depend largely on the gluten of flour proteins, which must absorb water before it can form into long elastic strands. A baker can control gluten for tenderness or firmness by selecting the appropriate flours and shortening, by the amount of liquid used, and by choice of mixing methods.

4. Dough or batter undergoes various stages in the baking process:

   - Formation and expansion of gases
   - Trapping of the gases in air cells
   - Coagulation of proteins
   - Gelatinization of starches
   - Evaporation of some of the water
   - Melting of shortenings
   - Browning of the surface and crust formation

5. **Staling**—the loss of moisture—can be slowed by protecting baked items from air, by adding fats and sugars to the formula to retain moisture, or by freezing baked items before they become stale.

   - Refrigeration speeds staling.
   - Crisp baked goods lose crispness when they absorb moisture from the air, so they should be stored in airtight wraps or containers.

6. The entire wheat kernel is ground for whole wheat flour, but bran (husk) and germ are removed for milling white wheat flour.

7. The function of fats in baking is to shorten gluten strands and to tenderize the product.

   - The three main types of shortenings are regular, emulsified, and shortening for puff pastry.
   - Butter and margarine add flavor to baked goods and they melt in the mouth, but doughs containing them are hard to handle because temperature makes them too hard or too soft.
   - Oils shorten too much to be used in baked goods except for some quick breads and cakes, and lard is seldom used today.

8. Sugars contribute flavor, texture, color, and moisture to baked products.

9. Liquid is needed in baking for gluten development and to aid leavening.

10. Eggs provide structure to baked goods, emulsify fats, aid in leavening, act as shortening, and provide moisture, flavor, nutritional value, and color.

11. The principal types of leaveners are yeast, chemical leaveners, air, and steam.

12. Salt, flavorings, and spices play important roles in baking.

    - Salt strengthens gluten structure and inhibits yeast growth.
    - The most important spices in the bakeshop are cinnamon, nutmeg, mace, cloves, ginger, caraway, cardamom, allspice, anise, and poppy seed.
    - Extracts are flavorful oils dissolved in oil.
    - Emulsions are flavorful oils mixed with water with the aid of emulsifiers.

Chapter 26 Exercises

1. Determine the percentages of each ingredient in the following recipe.

Ingredient	Weight	Percentage
Flour	4 pounds	
Sugar	4 pounds	
Baking powder	6 ounces	
Salt	4 ounces	
Shortening	1 pound 8 ounces	
Milk	2 pounds 4 ounces	
Eggs	2 pounds	

L.O. 26.2

2. Determine the amounts of each of the following recipe ingredients.

Ingredient	Weight	Percentage
Flour	6 pounds 8 ounces	
Sugar		100%
Baking powder		100%
Salt		7.5%
Shortening		2.9%
Milk		55%
Eggs		68%

L.O. 26.3

3. What is gluten? Why is it important in baking?

_____

_____

_____

L.O. 26.4

4. Name three ways to slow the staling of baked goods.

- _____

- _____

- _____

L.O. 26.6

5. Why might cooks prefer butter to shortening?

_____

_____

_____

L.O. 26.7

6. Indicate which of the following ingredients act as leaveners in baked products.

_____(1)   Air   _____(6)   Flour
_____(2)   Egg whites   _____(7)   Sugar
_____(3)   Cornstarch   _____(8)   Molasses
_____(4)   Steam   _____(9)   Baking soda
_____(5)   Baking powder   _____(10) Milk

L.O. 26.7

7. List five functions of fats in baked goods.

- _____

- _____

- _____

- _____

- _____

L.O. 26.7

8. What is meant by the expression "coagulation of proteins"? Explain its importance in the baking process.

_____

_____

_____

L.O. 26.5

133

Chapter 27 Exercises

1. Match each numbered step in yeast production with the lettered description or guideline that pertains to it.

    _____(1)   Scaling ingredients

    _____(2)   Mixing

    _____(3)   Fermentation

    _____(4)   Punching

    _____(5)   Scaling

    _____(6)   Rounding

    _____(7)   Benching

    _____(8)   Makeup and panning

    _____(9)   Proofing

    _____(10) Baking

    _____(11) Cooling

    _____(12) Storing

    a. Yeast acts on sugars and starches in the dough to produce carbon dioxide and alcohol.

    b. Dough is allowed to relax for 10 to 15 minutes.

    c. Shape dough into smooth, round balls.

    d. Common temperatures are between 400°F and 425°F (200°C and 220°C).

    e. Deflate the dough so that carbon dioxide is released.

    f. Wrapping cooled breads in moisture-proof bags retards staling.

    g. Dough is allowed a second fermentation period before baking.

    h. All ingredients must be weighed accurately.

    i. The seam should be centered on the pan's bottom to avoid splitting.

    j. Loaves should be removed from their pans and placed on racks.

    k. A properly developed dough should be smooth and elastic, not too sticky.

    l. Use a baker's scale to make each portion of dough uniform.

L.O. 27.1–27.3

2. Indicate one possible cause for each of the following bread-making problems.

(1) Poor shape

_____

_____

_____

(2) Crumbly

_____

_____

_____

(3) Crust too dark

_____

_____

_____

(4) Flat taste

_____

_____

_____

L.O. 27.1–27.3

3. Identify each of the following as a hard roll or bread product (HB), a soft roll product (S), a sweet dough product (SW), or a rolled-in dough product (R).

_____(1) Club roll   _____(6) Crescent roll
_____(2) Butterflake roll   _____(7) Knotted roll
_____(3) Wreath coffee cake   _____(8) Caramel roll
_____(4) Parker House roll   _____(9) Round loaf
_____(5) Cloverleaf roll   _____(10) Croissant

L.O. 27.1–26.3

Chapter 27 Check-in

1. Which of the following is not made from a rolled-in dough?

    A. Brioche
    B. Croissants
    C. Danish pastry
    D. None of the above are correct.

   L.O. 27.3

2. Which of the following is made from a rich dough?

    A. Focaccia
    B. Soft rolls
    C. Brioche
    D. White pan bread

   L.O. 27.2

3. The action of yeast in a mixed dough is called

    A. gluten formation.
    B. fermentation.
    C. punching.
    D. development.

   L.O. 27.1–27.3

4. After rolls and loaves are shaped, they are put in a warm place to rise. What is this rising process called?

    A. Punching
    B. Fermentation
    C. Oven spring
    D. Proofing

   L.O. 27.1–27.3

5. Which of the following is not one of the three basic building blocks of bread?

    A. Flour
    B. Yeast
    C. Sugar
    D. Water

   L.O. 27.1

CHAPTER 28

QUICK BREADS

Learning Objectives

After reading this chapter, you should be able to:

28.1   Prepare baking powder biscuits and variations.

28.2   Prepare muffins, loaf breads, coffee cakes, and corn breads.

28.3   Prepare popovers.

Chapter 28 Study Outline

1. The short preparation time for tender quick breads is possible because they involve little gluten development and they are leavened by chemical leaveners and steam, not yeast.
    - Chemical leaveners are too weak to make a light product if the gluten is too strong.
    - Popovers need a strong structure because they are leavened only by steam, so the batter is made with bread flour and is mixed well to develop the gluten.
2. Dough mixtures for quick breads are either soft doughs or batters.
3. Most quick breads are mixed by the muffin method.
4. Drop biscuits are mixed by the biscuit method, while some rich, cake-like muffins and coffee cakes are mixed by the creaming method.

Chapter 28 Exercises

1. What is the difference between the two types of batter?

_____

_____

_____

L.O. 28.2

5. Errors in mixing, scaling, baking, and cooling cakes cause many kinds of defects and failures.

6. Adjustments must be made to account for high altitudes when baking cakes.

7. Icings (frostings) and glazes on baked goods improve their appearance and flavor and form a coating that improves keeping quality.
   - Since fondant is hard to make, bakeshops nearly always purchase it prepared.
   - Buttercreams are popular icings used for many kinds of cakes.
   - Foam-type (boiled) icings are not stable and should be used quickly.
   - Flat icings are mixtures of ten parts sugar to one water.
   - Fudge-type icings are stable and hold up well on cakes and in storage.
   - Royal (decorator's) icing is used only for decorative icing.
   - Glazes are made from sugar or corn syrup or thinned fruit preserves.

8. In selecting icings, use heavy frostings for heavy cakes and light frostings for light cakes, best-quality flavorings, and coloring sparingly.

Chapter 29 Exercises

1. Match the cake mixing method with the item or description to which it corresponds.

   _____ (1) Creaming method
   _____ (2) Chiffon method
   _____ (3) Sponge method
   _____ (4) Prepared mixes
   _____ (5) Two-stage method

   a. Uses modern high-ratio shortenings
   b. Contains all ingredients except water and sometimes egg
   c. Standard method for mixing butter cakes
   d. Requires slightly firmer whipped egg whites than angel food cakes
   e. Most frequent cause of failure is insufficient whipping of the eggs and sugar

L.O. 29.1

2. Angel food cakes do *not* contain which type of ingredient?

   _____

L.O. 29.1, 29.3

142

3. a. Adding too much sugar to a cake batter is likely to lead to what three problems?

    * _____

    * _____

    * _____

    b. Baking a cake in an oven that is too hot is likely to lead to what three problems?

    * _____

    * _____

    * _____

L.O. 29.3

4. What physical phenomenon causes changes in altitude to affect cake baking?

    _____

    _____

    _____

L.O. 29.3

5. Match each numbered icing with the lettered description to which it applies.

    _____(1) Buttercream

    _____(2) Fudge-type

    _____(3) Foam-type

    _____(4) Royal

    _____(5) Fondant

    _____(6) Flat

    a. Sugar syrup crystallized to a smooth white mass
    b. Meringue made with a boiling syrup
    c. Heavy, cooked icing made like candy
    d. Also called decorator's icing
    e. Light, smooth mixture of fat and confectioners' sugar
    f. Mixture of ten parts sugar to one part water

L.O. 29.4

6. Low-fat cakes like genoise can be dry and firm because of their low shortening content. What technique is used to supply moistness to genoise cake layers?

_____

_____

_____

L.O. 29.2, 29.5

Chapter 29 Check-in

1. Which of the following cake-mixing methods is not appropriate for low-fat or foam cakes?

   A. Angel food method
   B. Chiffon method
   C. Creaming method
   D. Sponge method

   L.O. 29.1–29.3

2. Which of the following cake mixing methods is not appropriate for high-fat cakes?

   A. Sponge method
   B. Two-stage method
   C. Blending method
   D. Creaming method

   L.O 29.1–29.3

3. The development of the two-stage mixing method was made possible by which of the following?

   A. High-speed mixers
   B. Modern ovens
   C. Specially milled cake flours
   D. Emulsified or high-ratio shortenings

   L.O. 29.1

4. Cakes made for long-term display are usually decorated with

   A. buttercream.
   B. fondant.
   C. royal icing.
   D. fudge icing.

   L.O. 29.4, 29.5

5. Which of the following statements about icing cakes is false?

   A. Cupcakes can be iced with a spatula or dipped in soft icing.
   B. In general, use heavy icings with heavy cakes and light icings with light cakes.
   C. Use flavorings sparingly. The flavor of the icing should not be stronger than the flavor of the cake.
   D. Although sheet cakes require little labor to bake, ice, and decorate, they have limited use because they keep for only a short period of time if they are left uncut.

   L.O. 29.5

CHAPTER 30

Learning Objectives

After reading this chapter, you should be able to:

30.1   List the factors responsible for crispness, softness, chewiness, and spread in cookies.

30.2   Demonstrate the three basic cookie mixing methods.

30.3   Prepare the seven basic cookie types: dropped, bagged, rolled, molded, icebox, bar, and sheet.

30.4   Prepare pans for, bake, and cool cookies.

Chapter 30 Study Outline

1. In order to produce cookies with the desired shape, texture, and other characteristics, cooks need to know what causes various qualities.

2. Cookies do not contain much liquid, so gluten develops less during mixing than in many other baked products.

3. One-stage, creaming, and sponge methods are used for mixing cookies.

4. Cookies can be classified by the makeup methods used in their preparation.

    *   All cookies should be of uniform size and thickness.

    *   Dropped cookies are made from soft dough.

    *   Bagged or pressed cookies are made from dough soft enough to force through a bag tip but stiff enough to hold a shape.

    *   Rolled cookies are made from stiff dough.

    *   Molded cookies are formed by hand, by flattening with a weight or in special molds.

    *   Icebox (refrigerator) cookies can be prepared ahead of time and stored to bake freshly as needed.

    *   Bar cookies are baked in strips and cut while still warm from the oven.

    *   Dough for sheet cookies is spread in a sheet pan and cut after baking.

5. Most cookies are baked at a relatively high temperature for a short time.

CHAPTER 31

PIES AND PASTRIES

Learning Objectives
After reading this chapter, you should be able to:

31.1   Prepare flaky pie dough and mealy pie dough.

31.2   Prepare crumb crusts and short, or cookie, crusts.

31.3   Assemble and bake pies.

31.4   Prepare the following pie fillings: fruit fillings using the cooked juice method, the cooked fruit method, and the old-fashioned method; custard or soft fillings; cream pie fillings; and chiffon fillings.

31.5   Prepare puff pastry dough and puff dough products.

31.6   Prepare éclair paste and éclair paste products.

31.7   Prepare standard meringues and meringue desserts.

31.8   Prepare the following fruit desserts: cobblers, crisps, and bettys.

Chapter 31 Study Outline

1. Proper mixing of flour and shortening, and attention to gluten development are essential to successful production of pie crust.

    - Pastry flour and regular hydrogenated shortening alone or mixed with butter are the best choices. Liquid must be added cold.

    - During mixing and makeup, pie dough should be kept cool for the best blending of shortening and to retard gluten development.

    - Fat blended into the flour until particles are very small produces mealy pie dough; leaving the fat particles larger makes flaky dough.

    - Crumb crusts are suitable only for pies that do not require baking.

    - Short-dough crust is made from a type of cookie dough and is used mainly for small fruit tarts.

2. Baked pies include those with custard-type fillings in a single crust (soft pies) and those with fruit fillings and a second, top crust.

3. Unbaked pies are made by filling already-baked pie shells or crumb crusts with a prepared filling.

4. A variety of starches can be used to thicken cream and fruit pie fillings.

5. The greatest difficulty in cooking soft pies is cooking the crust completely without overcooking the filling.

6. The difference between puddings and cream pie fillings is that cream pie fillings are made with cornstarch.

7. Chiffon fillings are made by adding gelatin to a cream filling or to a thickened fruit and juice mixture.

8. Puff pastry is made up of many layers of fat sandwiched in between layers of dough.

9. Eclairs and cream puffs are made from an easy-to-prepare dough called eclair paste.

10. Meringues are beaten egg whites sweetened with sugar. The three types of basic meringues are common, Swiss, and Italian.

11. Fruit desserts include cobblers, crisps, and bettys.

Chapter 31 Exercises

1. What makes the difference between a flaky pie dough and a mealy pie dough?

_____

_____

_____

L.O. 31.1

2. Can trimmings from pie dough be used along with fresh dough? Why or why not?

_____

_____

_____

L.O. 31.1

3. What type of starch is most often used in:
   (1) Cream pies?

   _____

   (2) Fruit pies?

   _____

   (3) Fruit fillings that do not need to be cooked?

   _____

   (4) Pies that are to be frozen?

   _____

L.O. 31.4

4. Identify the differences between each of the following terms.
   (1) Cream pie fillings and puddings

   _____

   _____

   _____

   (2) Eclair paste and popover batter

   _____

   _____

   _____

L.O. 31.4, 31.6

5. What leavener causes puff pastry dough to rise when baked?

   _____

   _____

   _____

L.O. 31.5

6. What are the two ingredients of a common meringue?
   • _____

   • _____

L.O. 31.7
7. What is baked Alaska?

150

_____

_____

_____

L.O. 31.7

8. Assume you have made a fruit pie filling by the cooked juice method. At about what temperature should the filling be when the pie shell is filled?

_____

_____

_____

L.O. 31.3

Chapter 31 Check-in

1. Which of the following is an accurate description of cutting in the fat for flaky pie dough?

    A. The fat is cut in and blended with the flour until the mixture is smooth.

    B. The fat is cut into the flour until the mixture looks like cornmeal.

    C. The fat is cut into the flour until the lumps of fat are about the size of peas.

    D. The fat is rolled into the dough and the dough is then given three 3-folds.

L.O. 31.2

2. What are the main ingredients in a crumb crust?

    A. Crumbs, sugar, ice water

    B. Crumbs, sugar, melted butter

    C. Crumbs, pastry flour, butter

    D. Crumbs, butter, leavening

L.O. 31.3

3. Which of the following is the best starch to use for fruit pie fillings?

    A. Cornstarch

    B. Waxy maize

    C. Pastry flour

    D. Instant starch

L.O. 31.4

4. What is the primary leavening agent in éclair paste?

    A. Baking powder

    B. Baking soda

    C. Steam

    D. Air

L.O. 31.6

5. What is the primary leavening agent in puff pastry?

    A. Baking powder

    B. Baking soda

    C. Steam

    D. Air

L.O. 31.5

CHAPTER 32

CREAMS, CUSTARDS, PUDDINGS, FROZEN DESSERTS, AND SAUCES

Learning Objectives

After reading this chapter, you should be able to:

32.1   Cook sugar syrups to the seven stages of doneness.

32.2   Prepare vanilla custard sauce, pastry cream, and baked custard.

32.3   Prepare starch-thickened puddings and baked puddings.

32.4   Prepare bavarians, chiffons, mousses, and dessert soufflés.

32.5   Assemble parfaits, sundaes, and bombes.

32.6   Prepare dessert sauces.

Chapter 32 Study Outline

1. Simple syrup is a solution of equal weights of sugar and water.
    - Graininess results when cooked sugar crystallizes rather than staying dissolved in the syrup.
    - Testing the temperature with a candy thermometer is the best way to determine the stage of doneness.
2. Vanilla custard sauce, pastry cream, and baked custard are all classified as custards because they consist of a liquid thickened by the coagulation of eggs.
3. Starch-thickened puddings include cornstarch puddings (blanc mange) and cream puddings.
4. Baked puddings are custards that contain additional ingredients, usually in large quantities.
5. Bavarians, chiffons, mousses, and soufflés all have a light, fluffy or puffed texture created by the addition of whipped cream and/or egg whites.

6. Frozen desserts include ice cream, sherbet, and still-frozen desserts.
   - Few foodservice establishments make their own ice cream.
   - When purchasing ice cream, be aware of quality factors, such as smoothness, overrun, and mouth feel.
   - Popular ice cream desserts include parfaits, sundaes, bombes, meringue glacée, baked Alaska, and frozen eclairs.
7. Most dessert sauces fall into three categories:
   - Custard sauces
   - Fruit purées
   - Syrups

Chapter 32 Exercises

1. What are the two ingredients of a simple syrup?

   - _____

   - _____

L.O. 32.1

2. What is a custard?

   _____

   _____

   _____

L.O. 32.2

3. Name three of the four ingredients in a crème anglaise.

   - _____

   - _____

   - _____

L.O. 32.2

4. What is blanc mange?

_____

_____

_____

L.O. 32.3

5. What ingredient, if measured inaccurately, can make a bavarian runny or rubbery?

_____

L.O. 32.4

6. What is the difference between ice cream and sherbet?

_____

L.O. 32.5

7. Match each dessert on the left with its description on the right.

_____(1) Parfait
_____(2) Coupe
_____(3) Bombe
_____(4) Granité
_____(5) Sorbet

a. Alternating layers of ice cream and fruit or topping in a tall glass
b. Coarse, flavored ice
c. Molded and refrozen ice cream
d. Mixture made from fruit juice, water, and sugar
e. One or two scoops of ice cream topped with a syrup, fruit, or other topping

L.O. 32.5

Chapter 32 Check-in

1. Which of the following would not help prevent crystallization in cooked syrups?

    A. Adding a teaspoon of sugar crystals
    B. Adding corn syrup
    C. Washing down the sides of the saucepan with a brush dipped in water
    D. Covering the pan when the syrup first comes to a boil and allowing it to boil for several minutes.

    L.O. 32.1

2. When cooking crème anglaise, never heat it above

    A. 140°F (60°C).
    B. 165°F (74°C).
    C. 185°F (85°C).
    D. 212°F (100°C).

    L.O. 32.2

3. Which of the following types of puddings is heavier and more filling than the other three?

    A. Boiled
    B. Baked
    C. Steamed
    D. Starch-thickened

    L.O. 32.3

4. What ingredient is used to give Bavarians, mousses, chiffons, and soufflés their light texture?

    A. Whipped cream
    B. Whipped egg whites
    C. Both whipped cream and whipped egg whites used together
    D. All of the above are correct.

    L.O. 32.4

5. Which of the following desserts always contain at least two flavors of ice cream or sherbet?

    A. Bombes
    B. Parfaits
    C. Sundaes
    D. Baked Alaska

    L.O. 32.5

Practice Test

This Practice Test contains 80 multiple-choice questions that are similar in content and format to those found on the National Restaurant Association Educational Foundation's final exam for this course. Mark the best answer to each question by circling the appropriate letter. Answers to the Practice Test are on page 165 of this Student Workbook.

1. In operations too small to employ an executive chef, the person in charge of the kitchen is called a
   A. chef de partie.
   B. sous chef.
   C. station chef.
   D. working chef.
   L.O. 1.2

2. Generally, disease-producing bacteria grow best when the environment is
   A. neutral or nearly neutral.
   B. very cold.
   C. highly acidic.
   D. very dry.
   L.O. 2.1

3. The best way to cool a stock pot of soup is to
   A. take it off the range top to cool for one hour and then refrigerate it.
   B. let it cool completely at room temperature and then refrigerate it.
   C. set the pot in ice water, stir to cool, and then refrigerate it.
   D. place it in the refrigerator as soon as it finishes cooking.
   L.O. 2.1

4. Cross-contamination refers to
   A. the movement of bacteria from one food to another or from work surfaces or equipment to food.
   B. soil or bacteria transferred between kitchen departments.
   C. employees infecting each other with bacteria.
   D. people getting bacteria from animals or animal products.
   L.O. 2.1

5. Most cooking utensils in foodservice kitchens are made of
   A. stainless steel.
   B. cast iron.
   C. aluminum.
   D. copper.
   L.O. 3.1

6. A palette knife is used mainly for
   A. slicing soft fruits.
   B. trimming raw meats.
   C. cutting and serving pies.
   D. scraping bowls and icing cakes.
   L.O. 3.1

7. The heat transfer process from pan to food is called
   A. conduction.
   B. convection.
   C. radiation.
   D. wave action.
   L.O. 4.1

8. Which of the following methods is best for loosening the skin of tomatoes for easy peeling?

    A. Blanching
    B. Braising
    C. Poaching
    D. Steaming

L.O. 4.4, 4.5

9. Which of the following is not part of the sauté cooking method?

    A. Preheat the pan.
    B. Avoid overcrowding the pan.
    C. Prepare raw meat pieces by dusting with flour.
    D. Add a small amount of liquid and cover to finish cooking.

L.O. 4.5

10. Which of the following formulas determines the portion cost of a recipe?

    A. Cost of ingredients ÷ Number of portions
    B. Number of portions ÷ Cost of ingredients
    C. Hidden costs ÷ Cost of ingredients
    D. Hidden costs ÷ Number of portions

L.O. 5.12

11. Which of the following combinations contains the best balance of flavor, texture, and appearance?

    A. Duchesse potatoes and puréed squash
    B. Cream of celery soup and broiled chicken breast
    C. Cucumbers in yogurt-garlic dressing and garlic bread
    D. Stuffed tomato appetizer and meatballs in herbed tomato sauce

L.O. 6.4

12. The nutrient most important as a source of energy is

    A. saturated fat.
    B. unsaturated fat.
    C. carbohydrate.
    D. protein.

L.O. 6.7

13. Pieces of minced vegetable are

    A. thin slices.
    B. about 1 inch square.
    C. chopped very fine.
    D. all the same size and shape.

L.O. 7.5

14. Which of the following refers to cutting leaves into fine shreds?

    A. Chiffonade
    B. Batonnet
    C. Julienne
    D. Allumette

L.O. 7.5

15. A reduced or concentrated stock used to flavor a sauce is called a
    A. bouquet garni.
    B. convenience base.
    C. glaze (or glace).
    D. mirepoix.
    L.O. 8.5

16. The thickening of egg yolks in a liaison occurs because
    A. egg proteins coagulate when heated.
    B. they easily emulsify with stirring.
    C. of the tempering action of butter or other fat.
    D. boiling produces a slight curdling action.
    L.O. 8.11

17. The texture of a roux should be
    A. stiff.
    B. pourable, like a thick batter.
    C. elastic with a glossy surface.
    D. thin, almost runny.
    L.O. 8.8

18. If held too long on a steam table, cornstarch-thickened sauces are likely to
    A. become too thick.
    B. become too thin.
    C. develop a starchy taste.
    D. darken.
    L.O. 8.10

19. Which of the following might fix curdled hollandaise sauce?
    A. Folding in a stiffly beaten egg white
    B. Beating in a teaspoon of cold water
    C. Reheating the sauce just until it begins to bubble
    D. Beating in two additional tablespoons of softened butter, added all at once
    L.O. 8.13

20. Which of the following is not ordinarily used in stock?
    A. Fresh parsley
    B. Bay leaves
    C. Salt
    D. Peppercorns
    L.O. 8.3

21. To make blond roux from white roux,
    A. add an egg yolk.
    B. cook the mixture on high heat.
    C. cook the mixture until the color darkens slightly.
    D. add a little flour that has been browned slightly in an oven.
    L.O. 8.8

22. A liaison contains
    A. butter and flour.
    B. egg yolks and cream.
    C. waxy maize, water, and butter.
    D. egg yolk, flour, and a concentrated stock.
    L.O. 8.11

23. The mixture of ingredients used to clarify a stock is called the

    A. clearmeat.
    B. collagen.
    C. mirepoix.
    D. sachet.
  L.O. 9.5

24. What is the best way to prepare pasta that is to be added to a clear soup?

    A. Cook separately and then add.
    B. Rinse dry pasta in cold water and add when vegetables are partially done.
    C. Parboil for 30 to 60 seconds, depending on size; drain; then add to the soup to finish cooking.
    D. Add dry pasta at the same time as the vegetable pieces, stirring frequently to prevent sticking.
  L.O. 9.6

25. The best and most important ingredient for beef consommé clearmeat is

    A. oxtails.
    B. beef backbone.
    C. beef shank (shin beef).
    D. well-trimmed beef rib bones.
  L.O. 9.5

26. To serve consommé cold and jelled, it is often necessary to

    A. add unflavored gelatin.
    B. decrease the mirepoix by half when preparing the stock.
    C. add an acid ingredient, such as lemon juice, to increase jelling.
    D. start the jelling process by adding ice cubes or crushed ice.
  L.O. 9.5

27. The yield grade of beef and lamb is based on the proportion of usable meat to

    A. water.
    B. fat.
    C. bone.
    D. all unusable portions.
  L.O. 10.2

28. Unlike wild venison, farm-raised venison is

    A. milder in flavor.
    B. lower in fat content.
    C. less moist.
    D. requires longer cooking because of connective tissue
  L.O. 10.7

29. To reduce the baking time for spareribs

    A. cover the roasting pan.
    B. cut the ribs into small portions.
    C. increase the cooking temperature.
    D. simmer for 30 minutes before baking.
  L.O. 11.1

30. Although some chefs add mirepoix when roasting meat, others do not because

    A. the mirepoix's vegetable fibers cloud the jus.
    B. the mirepoix dries out and creates too strong a flavor.
    C. moisture from the vegetables creates steam around the roast.
    D. sugars from the vegetables cause the roast to brown excessively.
  L.O. 11.1

31. When making shish kebab, cooks often broil vegetables on separate skewers rather than on the same skewer with meat because

   A. contrasting flavors are kept apart.
   B. sodium content can be lowered.
   C. the marinade causes vegetables to wilt.
   D. cooking times are more controllable.

   L.O. 11.2

32. Which of the following tastes most like chicken?

   A. Pheasant
   B. Squab
   C. Partridge
   D. Quail

   L.O. 12.4

33. Which of the following specialty poultry items most closely resembles venison or lean beef?

   A. Emu
   B. Partridge
   C. Quail
   D. Rabbit

   L.O. 10.7, 12.4

34. How should you prepare giblets for inclusion in dressing?

   A. Chop and add uncooked to other ingredients.
   B. Cook completely before adding to other ingredients.
   C. Pan brown lightly to partially cook before adding.
   D. Parboil for 1 to 2 minutes depending on size and then chop and add while still warm.

   L.O. 13.8

35. At what temperature should you roast a 25-pound turkey?

   A. 180°F (82.2°C)
   B. 250°F–325°F (121.1°C–163°C)
   C. 325°F–375°F (163°C–190.5°C)
   D. 400°F–425°F (204.5°C–218.5°C)

   L.O. 13.1

36. Which of the following is a reliable method of testing for the doneness of an 8-pound roasted duck?

   A. Move a leg to see if it is loose at the joint.
   B. Insert a thermometer into the breast—it should read at least 180°F (82.2°C).
   C. Look for juices inside the cavity that are cloudy and dark.
   D. Insert a fork into the breast and thigh, twisting slightly to see if the pink color is gone from the flesh.

   L.O. 13.1

37. Most fish sticks are made from which fish?

   A. Cod
   B. Turbot
   C. Mackerel
   D. Ocean perch

   L.O. 14.6

38. Which of the following saltwater fish is classified as lean?

   A. Mackerel
   B. Ocean perch
   C. Salmon
   D. Swordfish

   L.O. 14.6

39. Why are oysters and clams often baked on a layer of rock salt?

    A. For seasoning
    B. To prevent them from tilting
    C. For an oven-to-table presentation
    D. To prevent smoking caused by runover juices

L.O. 15.1

40. Which of the following will probably need to be turned during broiling?

    A. Porgy fillets
    B. Whole 3/4-pound lobster
    C. Swordfish steak
    D. Shrimp sized 16–20 per pound

L.O. 15.2

41. The term *al dente* refers to

    A. degree of doneness.
    B. cooking with oil.
    C. serving with a sauce.
    D. garnishing with fresh herbs.

L.O. 16.2

42. Broccoli cooked with which of the following is likely to cause it to become mushy?

    A. Sugar
    B. Vinegar
    C. Baking soda
    D. Lemon juice

L.O. 16.1

43. Chlorophyll is responsible for which color in vegetables?

    A. White
    B. Red
    C. Yellow
    D. Green

L.O. 16.1

44. How many 2-ounce servings of green beans will be prepared from 8 pounds AP weight of fresh green beans?

    A. 56
    B. 76
    C. 112
    D. 128

L.O. 16.4

45. A yellow or gray color in freshly-cooked cauliflower is probably due to

    A. overcooking.
    B. undercooking.
    C. lack of freshness.
    D. acid in the cooking water or other ingredients.

L.O. 16.1

46. Which of the following would help tenderize carrots cooked in water?

    A. Longer cooking time
    B. Adding a little sugar at the beginning of cooking
    C. Adding a little orange juice at the beginning of cooking
    D. Adding a little vinegar part way through the cooking

L.O. 16.1

47. When should you add vegetables to the pan to sauté them?

    A. As soon as the fat is hot
    B. At the same time as the fat
    C. When the fat begins to sizzle
    D. When the fat just begins to smoke

L.O. 17.3

48. Which of the following should be simmered without a cover?

    A. Asparagus
    B. Carrots
    C. Beets
    D. Potatoes

    L.O. 16.1

49. Which cooking technique is similar to sautéing, except that the pan is not moved but the items being cooked are stirred and flipped?

    A. Pan-frying
    B. Braising
    C. Stir-frying
    D. Baking

    L.O. 17.3

50. The kind of rice used most often in foodservice operations is

    A. arborio.
    B. Basmati.
    C. instant.
    D. parboiled.

    L.O. 18.6

51. Which of the following should always be washed before cooking?

    A. Wild rice
    B. Instant rice
    C. Parboiled rice
    D. Converted rice

    L.O. 18.6

52. What is the main disadvantage to cooking rice in a large quantity of water?

    A. The grains get sticky.
    B. It is harder to drain.
    C. It is less fluffy.
    D. Nutrients are lost.

    L.O. 18.7

53. Which of the following menu items can most appropriately be served in the same meal?

    A. Coleslaw and sauerkraut
    B. Macaroni salad with peas and Spanish rice
    C. Tuna salad on lettuce and roast turkey with dressing
    D. Waldorf salad and baked ham

    L.O. 19.1

54. Although iceberg lettuce is a salad staple, its drawback is

    A. its cost.
    B. it loses crispness quickly.
    C. it bruises easily.
    D. lack of flavor.

    L.O. 19.2

55. Which of the following is most likely to interfere with the emulsification of mayonnaise?

    A. Room-temperature oil
    B. Too much oil
    C. Vinegar added to the egg yolks
    D. Eggs that are too fresh

    L.O. 19.10

56. A pullman loaf of bread is what shape?

    A. Plump, round
    B. Flat, round
    C. Long, oval
    D. Long, rectangular

    L.O. 20.1

57. Which of the following is important in assembling canapés?

    A. Using leftovers

    B. Whipping milk into the spreading butter

    C. Creating canapés while bases are still warm

    D. Using at least one ingredient with a pronounced flavor

L.O. 20.7

58. A green ring around the yolk of a hard-cooked egg is caused by

    A. lack of freshness.

    B. overcooking.

    C. cooking at low temperatures.

    D. starting the cooking in warm or hot water.

L.O. 21.3

59. Brewed coffee should be held no longer than

    A. one-half hour.

    B. one hour.

    C. two hours.

    D. three hours.

L.O. 21.14

60. Which garniture term refers to spinach?

    A. Florentine

    B. Jardinière

    C. Lyonnaise

    D. Princesse

L.O. 24.3

61. A brine for curing duck before smoking would not include

    A. potassium nitrate.

    B. curing salt.

    C. sugar.

    D. water.

L.O. 22.1, 22.2

62. What is the recommended maximum temperature for cold smoking?

    A. 85°F (30°C)

    B. 165°F (74°C)

    C. 200°F (93°C)

    D. 40°F (4°C)

L.O. 22.2

63. Which of the following is not one of the three basic types of forcemeats?

    A. Panada forcemeat

    B. Mousseline forcemeat

    C. Straight forcemeat

    D. Gratin forcemeat

L.O. 23.4

64. Why shouldn't you serve whipped potatoes, buttered cauliflower, and turkey breast slices together?

    A. There is not enough contrast in taste.

    B. They are the same pale color.

    C. Their textures are incompatible.

    D. The combination is not balanced nutritionally.

L.O. 24.2

65. Japanese dashi is a kind of

    A. fish.

    B. seaweed.

    C. stock.

    D. root vegetable.

L.O. 25.1

66. Paella is identified with which country?

A. Germany
B. Hungary
C. Italy
D. Spain

L.O. 25.2

67. The main purpose of fat in baked goods is to

A. leaven.
B. tenderize gluten.
C. coagulate proteins.
D. aid absorption of liquids.

L.O. 26.7

68. Strong flours are those high in

A. fat.
B. bran.
C. protein.
D. starch.

L.O. 26.4

69. The threefold procedure for rolled-in dough creates at least how many layers?

A. 7
B. 10
C. 50
D. 100

L.O. 27.3

70. An old dough is one that is

A. stale.
B. overhandled.
C. overfermented.
D. adequately fermented.

L.O. 27.1

71. Most quick bread batters are mixed by what method?

A. Muffin
B. Biscuit
C. Creaming
D. Two-stage

L.O. 28.2

72. Shortening used for the muffin method is

A. melted.
B. creamed with sugar and eggs.
C. cut into flour until pieces are pea-size.
D. cut into flour until the mixture has the texture of cornmeal.

L.O. 28.2

73. Cornstarch is sometimes used in sponge cakes for

A. tenderness.
B. strength.
C. springiness.
D. less absorption of fillings.

L.O. 29.3

74. For which kind of cake should you not grease the baking pan at all?

A. Angel food
B. Yellow sheet cake
C. Sponge layers
D. Pound cake

L.O. 29.3

75. Which cookie mixing method should be done in small batches?

A. One-stage
B. Two-stage
C. Creaming
D. Sponge

L.O. 30.2

76. Which of the following is likely to produce pale, dry cookies?

    A. Too low a temperature
    B. Overmixing
    C. Undergreasing the pan
    D. Opening the oven door during baking

L.O. 30.1

77. Compared to water, milk as the liquid for pie crust makes it

    A. flakier.
    B. saltier.
    C. tougher.
    D. brown more quickly.

L.O. 31.1

78. Which kind of pie should be baked at 325°F to 350°F (165°C to 175°C) for most of its cooking time?

    A. Pumpkin
    B. Apple, using the cooked fruit method
    C. Raisin, using the cooked fruit method
    D. Cherry, using the cooked juice method

L.O. 31.1

79. Cream pie fillings are usually a variety of

    A. custard sauce.
    B. pre-baked custard.
    C. bavarian cream.
    D. pastry cream.

L.O. 31.4

80. The fluffiness of dessert soufflés comes from

    A. beaten egg whites.
    B. beating the base ingredients.
    C. whipped cream.
    D. baking powder.

L.O. 32.4

Practice Test Answers and Text Page References

1.	D	p. 7	28.	A	p. 233	55.	B	p. 575
2.	A	p. 15	29.	D	p. 249	56.	D	p. 582
3.	C	p. 21	30.	C	p. 241	57.	D	pp. 594–595
4.	A	p. 22	31.	D	p. 262	58.	B	p. 614
5.	C	p. 42	32.	A	p. 302	59.	B	p. 639
6.	D	p. 47	33.	A	p. 302	60.	A	p. 702
7.	A	p. 53	34.	B	pp. 356–357	61.	A	p. 644
8.	A	p. 56	35.	B	p. 312	62.	A	p. 646
9.	D	p. 59	36.	A	p. 317	63.	A	p. 673
10.	A	p. 88	37.	A	p. 365	64.	B	p. 698
11.	B	pp. 96–97	38.	B	p. 360	65.	C	p. 718
12.	C	p. 100	39.	B	p. 400	66.	D	p. 751
13.	C	p. 114	40.	C	p. 399	67.	B	p. 761
14.	A	p. 118	41.	A	p. 431	68.	C	p. 763
15.	C	p. 133	42.	C	p. 433	69.	D	p. 785
16.	A	p. 139	43.	D	p. 433	70.	C	p. 776
17.	A	p. 136	44.	A	pp. 436–439	71.	A	p. 796
18.	B	p. 138	45.	A	p. 432	72.	A	p. 797
19.	B	p. 156	46.	A	p. 430	73.	A	p. 807
20.	C	p. 127	47.	A	p. 435	74.	A	p. 808
21.	C	p. 136	48.	A	p. 435	75.	D	p. 821
22.	B	p. 139	49.	C	p. 465	76.	A	p. 832
23.	A	p. 173	50.	D	p. 503	77.	D	p. 842
24.	A	p. 177	51.	A	p. 504	78.	A	p. 853
25.	C	p. 173	52.	D	p. 508	79.	D	p. 854
26.	A	p. 175	53.	D	p. 533, 557	80.	A	p. 878
27.	B	p. 212	54.	D	p. 534			

Chapter Check-in Answers

Chapter 1
1. B p.7
2. D p. 7
3. C pp. 9–10
4. D p. 5
5. A p. 7

Chapter 2
1. A p. 15
2. C P. 17
3. A p. 19
4. B p. 19
5. B p. 27

Chapter 3
1. A p. 33
2. A p. 37
3. D p. 38
4. B p. 38
5. B p. 45

Chapter 4
1. B p. 52
2. D p. 53
3. D p. 53
4. C pp. 54–55
5. A p. 56

Chapter 5
1. D p. 76
2. B p. 77
3. A p. 79
4. A p. 75
5. C p. 73

Chapter 6
1. D p. 93
2. B p. 92
3. B pp. 99–100
4. B p. 98
5. D pp. 96–97

Chapter 7
1. A p. 112
2. A p. 111
3. D p. 113
4. B p. 115
5. C p. 121

Chapter 8
1. A pp. 127–128
2. C p. 132
3. A p. 133
4. A p. 139
5. D p. 138

Chapter 9
1. A p. 170–171
2. D p171
3. C p. 173
4. B p. 177
5. A p. 172

Chapter 10
1. b p.210
2. C p. 212
3. C p. 227
4. A p. 213
5. B p. 221

Chapter 11
1. B p. 240–241
2. D p. 263
3. C p. 279
4. D p. 256
5. A p. 281

Chapter 12
1. C p. 298
2. A p. 301
3. A p. 303
4. C p. 303
5. B p. 303

Chapter 13
1. C p. 312
2. D p. 328
3. A p. 341
4. C p. 323
5. D p. 340

Chapter 14
1. C p. 360
2. C p. 360
3. D p. 360
4. A p. 369
5. C p. 377

Chapter 15
1. A p. 401
2. C p. 121
3. B p. 394
4. C p. 388
5. D p. 411

Chapter 16

1. C p. 431
2. B p. 431
3. A p. 433
4. B p. 444
5. C p. 448

Chapter 17

1. B p. 456
2. A p. 465
3. D p. 472
4. C p. 480
5. A p. 472

Chapter 18

1. D p. 486
2. C p. 487
3. A p. 491
4. C p. 501
5. B p. 503

Chapter 19

1. C p. 534
2. A p. 558
3. A p. 560
4. B p. 570
5. D p. 571

Chapter 20

1. A p. 582
2. D p. 583
3. D pp. 583–584
4. B p. 594
5. C p. 591

Chapter 21

1. C p. 612
2. C p. 623
3. D p. 628
4. B p. 629
5. C p. 638

Chapter 22

1. B p. 645
2. C p. 644
3. C p. 646
4. D p. 649
5. B p. 650

Chapter 23

1. B p. 668
2. A p. 669
3. B p. 674
4. D p. 674
5. A p. 676

Chapter 24

1. A p. 702
2. C pp. 698–699
3. B p. 708
4. D p. 711
5. C p. 714

Chapter 25

1. C p. 725
2. A p. 718
3. D p. 731
4. A p. 744
5. B p. 746

Chapter 26

1. C pp. 764–765
2. A p. 758
3. C p. 759
4. B p. 760
5. D p. 761

Chapter 27

1. A p. 790
2. C p. 774
3. B p. 776
4. D p. 777
5. C p. 773

Chapter 28

1. B p. 796
2. D p. 796
3. D p. 796
4. A p. 796
5. A p. 798

Chapter 29

1. C p. 804
2. A p. 805
3. D p. 804
4. C p. 821
5. D pp. 822–823

Chapter 30

1. C p. 828
2. A p. 829–830
3. D p. 829
4. A p. 831
5. A p. 832

Chapter 31

1. C p. 842
2. B p. 844
3. B p. 847
4. C p. 860
5. C p. 854

Chapter 32

1. A p. 870
2. C p. 871
3. C p. 874
4. D p. 877
5. A p. 887